Attainment's

Early Literacy Skills Builder

Level 3

Teacher's Guide

Diane Browder
Susan Gibbs
Lynn Ahlgrim-Delzell
Ginevra Courtade
Angel Lee

Early Literacy Skills Builder (ELSB) Teacher's Guide

Levels 2 and 3

Diane Browder • Susan Gibbs • Lynn Ahlgrim-Delzell • Ginevra Courtade • Angel Lee

Editing Linda Schreiber
Cover design Beverly Sanders
Cover illustration Jo Reynolds
Graphic design Elizabeth Ragsdale

ISBN: 1-94314-837-6
An Attainment Publication

Printed in the United States of America

Attainment Company, Inc.
PO Box 930160
Verona, WI 53593-0160
1-800-327-4269
www.AttainmentCompany.com

Contents

Overview

The **Building with Sounds and Symbols** lessons begin by teaching the concept of word (and general print) awareness. More complex emergent literacy skills are introduced and taught in a spiraling manner (e.g., objectives are repeated across levels). There are 5 lessons each in Levels 2 and 3. Each lesson takes approximately 60 minutes of daily instruction and is developed for small-group instruction. Lessons can be broken up into two 30-minute sessions during the instructional day. (Note that a portion of daily literacy should also be devoted to the **Building with Stories** component so that students receive about 90 minutes of literacy instruction daily.

Lessons in Levels Two and Three address key literacy components supported by the National Reading Panel (2000) and other professionals. The **Scope and Sequence** on pages 8–10 and 98–100 preceding each level details the skills.

Materials Needed to Teach

At the start of each lesson, a list of materials needed for the lesson is provided. This **Teacher's Guide** provides scripted text so that you know exactly what to say and do during the lesson. The purple text is the script that tells you what to say. The black text provides directions and general information. For each lesson, you'll need this Teacher's Guide and the **Student Response Book** manual. For students who are unable to point to the answers in the Student Response Book, the responses can be printed from Disc 1, cut apart, and laminated. The responses can be posted on Plexiglas® for student's who eye-gaze or made into laminated cards or strips for students who need to physically grasp the correct response. They can be mounted on augmentative or alternative communication (AAC) devices.

At the end of each lesson, students work on writing a book about themselves called "My Book About Me." The pages for this book can be copied from Appendix D of the **ELSB Implementation Guide** or can be printed from the PDF on Disc 1.

Preparing to Teach the Lessons

To prepare to teach the lessons, it is important to read and practice the script in advance. Some parts of the lesson will require a preplanning decision. For example, will the student respond using a verbal response or by pointing to the answers? Will response options need to be put on a Plexiglas® board for an eye-gaze response? If students will be using an AAC device, this should be preprogrammed. Note that art for use as AAC overlays is provided in Appendix H of the ELSB Implementation Guide and on Disc 1.

Teaching the Lesson

Begin a lesson by engaging the students with the Lesson Opening. Follow by teaching Objective 1, followed by Objective 2, and so on in succession until all objectives for the lesson have been taught. Some teachers choose to complete Objective 14, the writing activity, at another time of day if students require a break. They also devote another 30 minutes to reading classroom literature for the Buildings with Stories component of ELSB.

Lessons should be repeated as needed for students to begin making independent responses. Students do not need to master a lesson before moving on to the next lesson; however, repeating the lessons helps students begin to respond independently. Some teachers find it helpful to follow a pattern for lesson repetition by devoting, for example, 2, 4, or 10 days to each lesson before moving on to the next lesson.

Advancing to the Next Level

Each level of the Building with Sounds and Symbols component has an **Assessment Manual.** The corresponding assessment should be used to determine the student's mastery of skills before proceeding to the next level. Once the student has proceeded through the end of a level, administer the assessment to the student individually to determine if the student is ready to progress to the next level. A mastery level should be determined for each student individually; a minimum of 75% mastery may be adequate for some students. If a student does not obtain the mastery level determined for him or her, repeat the lessons in the level and readminister the assessment. For students who seem to be "stuck" on a level due to lack of mastery of a particular skill (e.g., not reaching mastery on two attempts), consider two alternatives. First, consider increasing the number of days devoted to each lesson. Second, proceed to the next level for skills that are spiraled back in and repeated at the upper level. Review the full Scope and Sequence of the ELSB program (included in Appendix A in the ELSB Implementation Guide) to determine if a particular skill is reviewed at an upper level.

Level 2

Level 2 Scope and Sequence

Objective	Activity	Lesson 1	Lesson 2	Lesson 3	Lesson 4	Lesson 5
1. Read sight words using time-delay instruction	Flashcard Game	me, is, friend	me, is, friend	me, is, friend	me, is, friend	me, is, friend
2. Point to the sight words to complete sentences	Flashcard Game	Show me the picture, please. Kathy is happy. Randy is my friend.	He sat next to me. The book is on the table. I am going to see my friend.	Give the ball to me, please. Where is my hat? Kevin has a new friend.	My mom loves me. My friend is happy. She is at school.	Please show me! Ms. Grey is my teacher. Monique is her friend.
3. Point to text as it is read	Pointing to Words	Read "Moe Is Not Happy." Students point to text in lines 1–2.	Read "Moe Is Not Happy." Students point to text in lines 5–6.	Read "Moe Is Happy." Students point to text in lines 1–3.	Read "Moe Is Happy." Students point to text in lines 4–6.	Read "Moe Is Not Happy." Read "Moe Is Happy." Students point to text in lines 7–10 "Moe Is Happy."
4. Say and/or point to a word to complete a repeated story line	Hidden Words	Repeated word: down	Repeated word: crown	Repeated word: frog	Repeated word: today	Repeated word: sings

Objective	Activity	Lesson 1	Lesson 2	Lesson 3	Lesson 4	Lesson 5
5. Respond to literal questions about a story	Answering Questions	"Moe Is Not Happy" Line 1: Who is Moe? Line 4: Is Moe happy or sad? Line 5: Where does Moe jump? Line 9: What does Moe want?	"Moe Is Not Happy" Line 2: Is Moe happy every day? Line 4: Who is sad? Line 7: What does Moe say? Line 10: What does Moe do?	"Moe Is Happy" Line 4: Is Moe sad today? Line 6: Who came to play? Line 7: Who sings? Line 10: Who is happy?	"Moe Is Happy" Line 1: Who is Moe's friend? Line 2: What kind of frog is Molly? Line 6: What did Molly come to do? Line 8: Who sings?	"Moe Is Not Happy" Line 9: What does Moe want? Line 10: What does Moe do? "Moe Is Happy" Line 6: Who came to play with Moe? Line 10: Who is happy?
6. Demonstrate understanding of syllable segmentation by clapping out syllables in words	Chunking Words	2–3 syllables: happy teacher's name students' names	2–3 syllables: hello students' names jumping	2–3 syllables: Molly happy jumping	2–3 syllables: happy hello today	2–3 syllables: Molly jumping teacher's name students' names
7. Demonstrate understanding of phoneme segmentation by tapping out sounds in CVC words	Tapping Out Sounds					
8. Identify letter-sound correspondences	Letter Sounds Game	/a/ and /m/	/a/ and /m/	/s/, /a/, /m/	/s/, /a/, /m/	/s/, /a/, /m/

(Continued on next page)

Level 2 Scope and Sequence *(continued)*

Objective	Activity	Lesson 1	Lesson 2	Lesson 3	Lesson 4	Lesson 5
9. Point to and/ or say the first/last sounds in words	First/Last Sound Game	at, man, mat, am	mat, at, as, man	sat, mat, sam, am	sat, at, sam, man	at, man, sam, am
10. Identify pictures that begin/end with given sounds	Finding Pictures with Special Sounds	alligator, man, mouse, apple	add, man, ant, mail	sick, alligator, milk, soup	mop, man, ant, sock	milk, man, ant, sock
11. Point to letter sounds in words	Stretching Words					
12. Blend sounds to identify pictures	Finding Pictures					
13. Point to pictures/words representing new vocabulary	The New Word Game	**happy, sad**	sad, happy	**mad,** happy	**scared,** mad	**excited,** scared
14. Use new vocabulary words and personal information to create a story	Fun with Writing	___ makes me happy.	___ makes me sad.	___ makes me mad.	___ makes me scared.	___ makes me excited.

Lesson 1

Materials

- Moe the frog puppet
- Sight word flashcards: me, is, friend
- 2" × 2" Post-it® notes
- **Level 2 Student Response Book** (pages 6–33)
- Magnetic dry erase board and marker
- **All About Moe** easel book: "Moe Is Not Happy" story
- Pictures of items that make the students happy
- Pencils, crayons, alphabetic rubber stamps, glue
- "My Book About Me" books completed by students in previous lessons
- "My Book About Me, _____ makes me happy" page in Appendix D
- Pictures of objects, actions, and events that make the students happy

Optional Materials

- AAC device
- Pointer/light pointer
- Plexiglas® for eye gazing
- Optional pictures or text for AAC device (see Appendix H):
  - Lesson Opening: Hello, Moe
  - Objective 4: down
  - Objective 14: _____ makes me happy.
  - Lesson Closing: Goodbye, Moe

Tips

- If needed, use the magnetic dry erase board and a marker (or magnetic objects) for reinforcement. Draw a line on the magnet board dividing it into two columns. At the top of the first column, place a picture of the student. At the top of the second column, place a picture of yourself. When a student responds appropriately, congratulate him or her for good work and place a mark on the student side. If a student does not respond appropriately, place a mark on your side. At the end of the lesson, count the marks and find out who had more for that day. Encourage students to participate by being enthusiastic about the marks they received.

- If a student requires an augmentative or alternative communication (AAC) device, preprogram it using the text from the optional materials list.

- All student materials (including AAC overlays and the "My Book About Me" pages) can be printed from Disc 1. Printing from the disc allows you to adapt the materials for students.

- If you are working with a student whose mode of responding is to eye-gaze, the student response options can be printed from Disc 1, laminated, and cut apart. The student choices can be adhered to Plexiglas® with Velcro®. Point to the correct answer after the student gazes to it to provide the watching peers with feedback.

▶ Lesson Opening

Engage the students by saying, **Good morning, Moe! Moe has been waiting all night to see you. Moe doesn't look very happy today. Are you sad today, Moe?** Have Moe woefully nod and whisper in your ear. **Oh, I see. You have been sad and now you want the boys and girls to help you be happy. Boys and girls, please say hello to Moe with a happy smile, because he has been sad today. Get ready . . . Hello, Moe! Great job, now say it by yourselves.** Have students use an AAC device if needed to say, "Hello, Moe." **Now I know you want to know why Moe is sad; but first we need to play our Flashcard Game. So we will review our words and then we will read a story about Moe.**

Objective 1

Read sight words using time-delay instruction

Activity

Flashcard Game

Materials

- Moe the frog puppet
- Sight word flashcards: me, is, friend

Tip

A constant time-delay procedure is used to promote near-errorless responding. If a student is making errors in Round 1, which is the 0-second time-delay round, he or she may need additional practice (outside of this lesson) in imitating your model of choosing the correct response. Using pictures, have the student practice pointing where you point until he or she can do so fluently. If the student makes mistakes in Round 2, which is the 5-second time-delay round, shorten the time before you show the correct answer to 2 seconds. He or she will only have time to answer if certain. The student may also need to practice "wait training" to wait for the response. To do "wait training," use several sheets of different colored paper and say, **Point to the paper.** Have the student wait for you to point to show him or her which sheet.

Instructions

Flashcard Game: Part I. Part I of the Flashcard Game will give students practice saying or pointing to words with guidance.

Round 1: In this round, point to the correct answer as you ask the student to point (0-second time delay).

Lay the sight word flashcards in front of the students. Introduce the activity: **Let's play a game. I'll point to a word, then you point to the same word. Watch me.**

me	is

friend

Move the sight word flashcards in front of the first student. Point to the sight word ______ while saying, **This word is ______. (Student name), now you point to ______.**

Be sure you are pointing to the sight word as you say the word. Don't move your finger until the student points to where you are pointing. If you know a student will not imitate you, guide his or her hand for correct responding. For students who eye-gaze, use a light pointer or tap the answer to get them to focus their gaze on the correct answer.

When the student points to ______, say, **Yes, ______.** For students who are verbal, also say, **What word?** and have them say the word.

Wonderful job pointing to the word ______!

Shuffle the sight word flashcards and display them in a new order in front of the next student. In this round, each student takes a turn pointing to the same sight word before moving on to the next sight word.

(Second student's name), point to ______. Be sure you are pointing to ______ as you say the word. Use the same prompt if required.

After each student's turn, shuffle the sight words around so they are not in the same position. Repeat shuffling sight words and pointing to the words until each student has had a turn with each word. Be sure all students are watching during each student's turn to encourage incidental learning.

Round 2: In Round 2 of the Flashcard Game, students point to or say the sight word independently. Moe is ready to help after giving the student up to 5 seconds to initiate a response (a 5-second time delay).

Have Moe whisper in your ear. **Okeydokey, Moe. We can do that. Moe wants you to find the word. He can help you if you are not sure. (Student's name), find the word ______.**

Allow the student 5 seconds to point to the word. After the student finds the word, have Moe point to the same word with the student. **(Student's name), you point with Moe. Thank you for helping, Moe.**

If the student is verbal, have him or her say the word also. If the student does not point, have Moe prompt the answer and restate the word.

Give each student a turn to practice pointing to the sight word you name. Shuffle the sight words and repeat the process for each student with the remaining words. Be sure all students are watching each other's turn.

Awesome playing the Flashcard Game! Moe is learning to read and so are you! Let's play the next game.

Assisting Students

Prompt If the student does not point to the word, use Moe to point to the correct word, saying, **Moe pointed to ______. Now you point to ______.** If the student still does not point, physically guide his or her hand.

Correction If the student points to the wrong word, model the correct response by pointing to the correct word and saying, **This is the word ______. Now you point to ______.** If the student still does not point to the correct word, physically guide his or her hand. Give a turn to another classmate, and praise that student for doing it correctly.

Pile on the Praise

Objective 2

Point to the sight words to complete sentences

Activity

Flashcard Game

Materials

- Moe the frog puppet
- Sight word flashcards: me, is, friend
- **Level 2 Student Response Book** (pages 6–11)

Instructions

Flashcard Game: Part II. Display the Student Response Book. Place Moe's mouth near your ear and appear to be intently listening. **Moe wants you to read your new word in a sentence. Moe, why do you need to read the words in sentences?** Place Moe's mouth near your ear again. **I see . . . that's what the "big frogs" do! The "big frogs" read words in sentences. Then that's what we want to do!**

Model reading sentence A.1 while pointing to each word in the sentence. Place *verbal emphasis* on the underlined word. **Show me the picture, please. Listen again. Show me the picture, please.**

Read sentence B.1, pointing to each word. **Show ______ the picture, please.** Point to the blank space.

Place the sight word flashcards in front of a student, using the correct answer and one distractor. **Show Moe which word goes here** (pointing to the blank space in the sentence). **What word goes here? ______ or ______?**

Allow the student 5 seconds to respond. If the student responds correctly, affirm by saying, **Yes, me. Show me the picture, please.**

Shuffle the sight words and repeat the script with sentences A.2 "**Kathy is happy**" and B.2, as well as sentences A.3 "**Randy is my friend**" and B.3.

Assisting Students

Prompt If the student does not respond within 5 seconds, read sentence A again, placing verbal emphasis on the sight word. Then read sentence B, pausing at the blank space.

______ is the word that goes here. I can find ______. Point to the correct sight word and say, **(Student's name), point to ______ with me. Yes, ______.**

Correction Do not allow students to practice incorrect responses. For a student who can point and is about to point to an incorrect response, physically guide his or her hand to the correct response while verbally reinforcing the response. For students who use eye-gaze and are visually attending to the incorrect response, remove the incorrect response and visually cue them to the correct response.

Objective 3

Point to text as it is read

Activity

Pointing to Words

Materials

- Moe the frog puppet
- "Moe Is Not Happy" story
- **Level 2 Student Response Book** (page 12)

Tips

- Use a wait time of 5 seconds for all responses in this activity. However, students may need longer than 5 seconds initially. In this case, responding within 5 seconds should be viewed as a goal to work toward. Note and track response time for any student for whom you feel it is physically difficult to respond within 5 seconds.
- The goal of text pointing in this level is to have students move left-to-right and top-to-bottom.
- Do not slow your speed of reading to accommodate students' speed of movement. Work toward having students keep pace with your speed of reading as they point to the text.

Instructions

Introduce the activity by saying, **Today we are going to read a new story, "Moe Is Not Happy."**

While displaying the book so all can see, read "Moe Is Not Happy" with enthusiasm, pointing to the text, moving left-to-right and top-to-bottom.

After reading the story, return to the text-pointing page. Say, **Now Moe needs help reading his story. You can help him. I want you to point to each word in the line that I read. Like this.** While displaying the book so all can see, read lines 1 and 2 of "Moe Is Not Happy." Point to each word in lines 1 and 2 as you read. Then choose a student to point. Students can point to the text in the story, or you can use the page in the Student Response Book.

(Student's name), your turn! Point to the words for Moe as I read the line. I'm going to show you where to start, and I want you to follow along by pointing to each word as I read it. Show the student where to start pointing by touching the first word.

Repeat for each student, using the lines in the book (or in the Student Response Book).

Let's find out what Moe wants to do next!

Assisting Students

Prompt Modeling for the correct response is already built into the script. A student is given 5 seconds to begin responding. If the student does not initiate a response within 5 seconds, provide a visual cue. A visual cue may be tapping the page in the book and modeling the pointing. If there is still no response within 5 seconds, physically guide the student's hand to point to the words.

Objective 4

Say and/or point to a word to complete a repeated story line

Activity

Hidden Words

Materials

- Moe the frog puppet
- "Moe Is Not Happy" story (prepare for this activity by adhering a Post-it® note to cover the word *down* highlighted in yellow in story line 6)
- **Level 2 Student Response Book** (page 13)

Tips

- For students who eye-gaze, print the student page from Disc 1 and cut the choices apart. Place the choices a distance apart so that you can discriminate the students' purposeful choices.

- If a student is unable to verbalize, program the AAC device to say the hidden word. Let the student activate the AAC device to say the hidden word and to choose the picture representing the hidden word.

Instructions

Have Moe whisper to you. **Let's play the Hidden Words game! I am going to read a line from the "Moe Is Not Happy" story, and I will point to a word that is hidden** (covered with the Post-it® note). **Get ready!**

Read line 5 from "Moe Is Not Happy," emphasizing the word *down*.

Read line 6, pausing to remove the Post-it® note. Point to the word *down* and say, **Down.**

Again, cover the word *down* in line 6. Say, **It's your turn, boys and girls! I am going to read these lines, and this time I want you (or a student's name) to say the hidden word. Get ready!**

Read lines 5 and 6, pausing for a student to indicate the hidden word *down* in line 6. Uncover the word when students say it. Repeat until all students have had a turn.

Now Moe wants you to point to the picture and the word that tells what the hidden word was. First Moe is going to show you how to do it, and then you will have a turn. I will read the lines again, and he will point to a picture that tells what the uncovered word is. He has two choices here.

Point to the pictures in the Student Response Book and tell the students what the two choices are. Read lines 5 and 6 again, pausing on line 6 for Moe to point to the picture/word representing *down*. Encourage students to say the uncovered word (use an AAC device for nonverbal students). Repeat the sequence for each student.

Assisting Students

Prompt If there is no response within 5 seconds, provide the student with a visual cue. A visual cue might consist of tapping (or using a light pointer to point to) the correct response. Say the word as you give the visual cue. If there is still no response within 5 seconds, physically guide the student's hand to the correct response. Say the word as you give the physical cue.

Objective 5

Respond to literal questions about a story

Activity

Answering Questions

Materials

- Moe the frog puppet
- "Moe Is Not Happy" story
- **Level 2 Student Response Book** (pages 14–17)

Tips

- Each line is numbered in the story. In this activity, lines 1, 4, 5, and 9 are appropriate places to ask questions. When reading "Moe Is Not Happy," stop to ask questions at lines 1, 4, 5, and 9. You do not need to ask each student each question; rather, have students take turns answering the questions.
- For students who eye-gaze, print the student page from Disc 1 and cut the choices apart. Place the choices a distance apart so that you can discriminate the students' purposeful choices.

Instructions

Start by having Moe whisper to you. **Moe wants to hear his story again. But this time, I am going to ask you some questions about Moe. You are going to answer the questions by pointing to a picture. The answers are here.** Touch the page in the Student Response Book. **Get ready!**

Read the story "Moe Is Not Happy," stopping to ask the following questions at the end of the designated lines. After asking the question, point to and name the answer choices in the Student Response Book, and then ask the question again. Encourage students who are verbal to point to the correct response and to say the correct response.

Question 1 from Line 1: **Who is Moe?**
Question 2 from Line 4: **Is Moe happy or sad?**
Question 3 from Line 5: **Where does Moe jump?**
Question 4 from Line 9: **What does Moe want?**

Assisting Students

Prompt If there is no response within 5 seconds, provide the student with a visual cue. For this skill, you might ask Moe to do the visual prompt (e.g., say, **Moe, can you help [student's name] find the answer?**). A visual cue might consist of having Moe tap the correct response. Say, **Moe has shown you the answer. Now I will read the question again, and you show me the answer.** Read the question a second time. If there is still no response within 5 seconds, physically guide the student's hand to the correct response. Say the word as you give the physical cue.

Correction Do not allow students to practice incorrect responses. For a student who can point and is about to point to an incorrect response, physically guide his or her hand to the correct response while verbally reinforcing the response. For students who use eye-gaze and are visually attending to the incorrect response, remove the incorrect response and visually cue them to the correct response.

Objective 6

Demonstrate understanding of syllable segmentation by clapping out syllables in words

Activity

Chunking Words

Materials

- Moe the frog puppet

Tip

A great deal of thought must be given to how a student who is physically challenged will demonstrate this skill. When providing physical cues, make sure the cue can be faded over time. In order for the cue to be faded, the movement you choose must be one the student can create independently (e.g., don't use clapping as a physical cue if the student is unable to clap independently). One way to determine the best movement for the student to use would be to turn on some music, demonstrate moving to the music, and then watch to see what body part the student is able to move independently.

Instructions

Place Moe's mouth near your ear and appear to be listening intently. **Moe is very shy. He says words in a funny way. He says the sounds in words very slowly. Sometimes it is hard to figure out what he means. Moe wants us to help him. He wants to say the word *happy*. Okeydokey, Moe, you say *happy*.** Listen with concern as Moe says the word ***happy.***

Have Moe say, ***Ha...ppy,*** slowly dividing it into two syllables.

Moe said *happy* the slow way. He said *ha...ppy.* I think he is trying to tell us the syllables he hears in *ha...ppy.* Moe, say *happy* again and we'll clap out the syllables.

Model clapping out the two syllables in the word *happy* as Moe says the word. Make certain that Moe says *happy* slowly, clearly dividing the syllables as he speaks.

Have Moe say, ***Ha...ppy.***

Let's say *happy* again slowly and clap out the syllables for Moe. I'll clap and you help me. *Ha...ppy.* Help me do that again, boys and girls. Repeat the script.

Have Moe whisper in your ear. **Moe wants to try again with more words. Moe, you choose the next word!**

Have Moe say, **(your name).**

Repeat the above script using **your name** and some **students' names** that are two to three syllables in length.

Objective 8

Identify letter-sound correspondences

Activity

Letter Sounds Game

Materials

- Moe the frog puppet
- **Level 2 Student Response Book** (pages 18–20)

Tip

When a letter appears between two virgules (/ /), say the sound the letter makes rather than the letter name (e.g., /a/ means to make the sound the letter *a* says). Stretch the sound when multiple letters (e.g., /aaa/) appear within the virgules.

Instructions

Letter Sounds Game: Part I. Part I introduces the letter *a* and the sound short *a* makes. Introduce the activity: **We are going to play the Letter Sounds Game. It's a fun game. Here we go.**

Touch below the *a* on the Sound Presentation page in the Student Response Book and say, **This letter says /aaa/. This letter *a* says /aaa/. Touch /aaa/ with me**. Be sure you are pointing below the *a* as you say the sound. Don't move your finger until the student points to where you are pointing. **Your turn. Touch /aaa/**. Give each student an opportunity to touch the *a*.

Letter Sounds Game: Part II. Part II helps students discriminate the short *a* sound from one distractor. Introduce the activity: **Now we get to do the next page of the Letter Sounds Game. Get ready!**

Turn to the Letter-Sound Discrimination page in the Student Response Book. **Touch /aaa/. Good job touching /aaa/. The letter *a* says /aaa/.** Give each student an opportunity to touch the *a*.

Whether students are verbal or nonverbal, encourage them to make the sound for short *a*. **This time I will touch the *a* and you say the sound /aaa/. Ready?** Give each student an opportunity to say /a/.

Letter Sounds Game: Part III. Part III helps students identify and discriminate the short *a* sound when it is the beginning sound in words.

Turn to the Aggie and Ally page in the Student Response Book and say, **Our new sound is /aaa/. Let's practice. Touch /aaa/. Nice touching /aaa/. We are going to play a really fun game. First, we will listen to a poem about Aggie and Ally. Aggie and**

Ally are alligators and they love words that start with /aaa/. Let's read their poem and see if we can hear words that start with /aaa/.

Read the following poem one time. While you read, point to the *a* on the Aggie and Ally page each time you say a word that begins with short *a*.

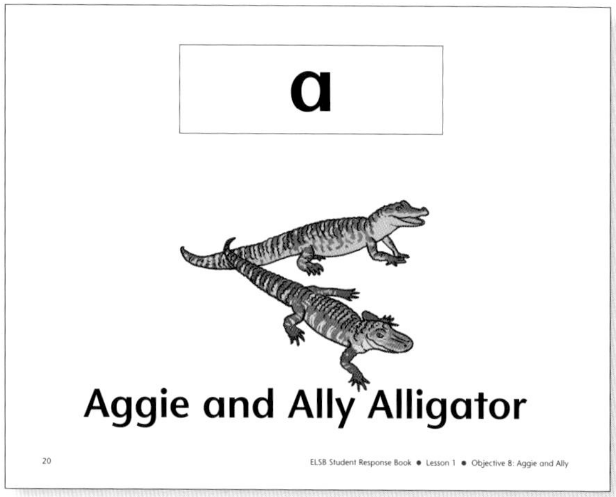

Aggie and Ally

Aggie the **a**lligator lives down in the bay
With her sister named **A**lly on
"**A**lligator Way."
Aggie **a**nd **A**lly work in the morning
And play in the **a**fternoon.
They play a game called "**A**fternoon Moon."
They swim up in the water **a**nd go snap, snap, snap.
They swim down in the water **a**nd go whap, whap, whap!
Then Aggie **A**lligator **a**nd **A**lly **A**lligator
Take a long, long **a**fternoon nap!

I will read the poem again and point to /aaa/ when I hear words that begin with /aaa/. This time you help me. You touch /aaa/ when you hear a word that starts with /aaa/.

Read the poem a second time and encourage students to listen and point to the *a* on the Aggie and Ally page when they hear words that begin with /a/. Stretch the beginning of the sound to emphasize the *a*. When a student touches the *a* at the appropriate time, give feedback and praise. For example: **Good. The first sound in alligator is /aaa/.** Note that students may find it difficult to point to the sound every time they hear it, but even pointing to the sound some of the time helps develop their phonemic awareness.

Assisting Students

Prompt If you know a student will not imitate you, guide his or her hand for correct responding. For students who eye-gaze, use a light pointer or tap the answer to get them to focus their gaze on the correct answer.

Correction Touch below the *a* and say, **This sound is /aaa/. Say /aaa/ with me. /aaa/. Say it by yourself. What sound?**

Objective 9
Point to and/or say the first/last sounds in words

Activity

First/Last Sound Game

Materials

- Moe the frog puppet
- **Level 2 Student Response Book** (page 21)

Tips

- When you say the word the "fast way," touch the colored smiley face to focus students, say "Ready," then slash under the word as you say it.
- Stretch the sound when multiple letters appear in the virgules (e.g., /aaa/). Note that some sounds cannot be stretched (e.g., /t/).

Instructions

Place Moe's mouth near your ear and appear to be listening. **Moe wants us to get really good at knowing the first sounds in words. Moe has a fun game to play with colored smiling faces to help us hear the first sounds in words. OK, Moe! We are ready to play the First/Last Sound Game.**

Touch the green smiley face on the student page. **Get ready to read the word that comes after the green smiley face. I'll touch and say the first sound /aaa/. Then I will touch and say the last sound /t/. Say the sounds in this word with me: /aaa/ /t/.**

I can say this word the fast way. Ready (put your finger on the smiley face, then say *at* without segmenting it into sounds), ***at*. Say this word the fast way with me, *at*. Yes, *at*. We said *at* the fast way.**

Touch the first sound in *at*. Say, **The first sound in *at* is /aaa/. Touch the first sound in *at*.** Have a student touch or point to the *a*.

Say the first sound in *at*. Place emphasis on the beginning sound when you say the word *at*. **Yes, /aaa/ is the first sound in the word *at*.**

Repeat the script above for: **man, mat, am,** changing the script to match the color of the smiley face and the beginning sound you are focusing on.

Assisting Students

Prompt If you know a student will not imitate you, guide his or her hand for correct responding. For students who eye-gaze, use a light pointer or tap the answer to get them to focus their gaze on the correct answer.

Correction Touch below each sound and say, **This sound is /___/. Say /___/ with me. /___/. Say it by yourself. What sound?**

Objective 10

Identify pictures that begin/end with given sounds

Activity

Finding Pictures with Special Sounds

Materials

- Moe the frog puppet
- **Level 2 Student Response Book** (pages 22–25)

Instructions

Place Moe's mouth near your ear and appear to be listening. **Moe is ready to play his game Finding Pictures with Special Sounds. The special sounds today are /mmm/ and /aaa/.**

Display the Student Response Book. Point to each picture as you name it (alligator, rose, vase, hat), placing emphasis on the first sound in each word.

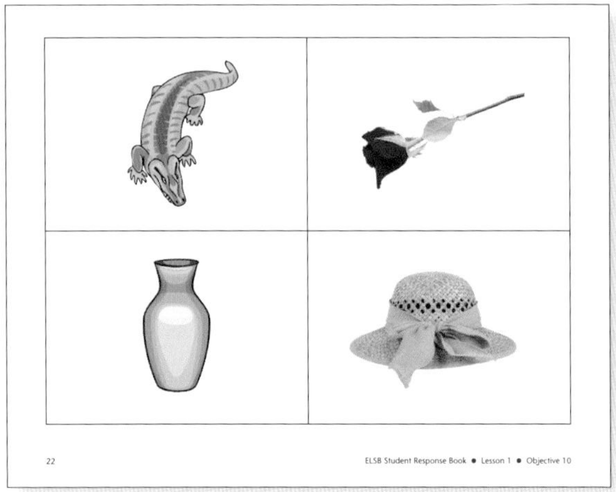

Say the picture words with me. The first sound in *alligator* is /aaa/. The first sound in *rose* is /rrr/. The first sound in *vase* is /vvv/. The first sound in *hat* is /h/.

Point to the picture that has /aaa/ as its first sound. Show me the picture that starts with /aaa/.

Have a student point to the alligator. **Yes, the first sound in the word *alligator* is /aaa/.**

Repeat the above script for each student page. Change the script to match the target sound. The target response (focusing on either /a/ or /m/) has an asterisk in the list below.

cap, rain, *man, dog
eye, leaf, house, *mouse
pie, *apple, fork, bird

Give all students 5 seconds to respond after you say, **Show me the picture that starts with ___.**

Assisting Students

Prompt and Correction

If there is no response within 5 seconds, point to the correct response and say, **The first sound in ___ is /___/. Touch the picture of ______.** If the student does not respond within 5 seconds, physically guide the student's hand to the correct response and say, ___ **starts with /___/.**

Objective 13

Point to pictures representing new vocabulary

Activity

The New Word Game

Materials

- Moe the frog puppet
- **Level 2 Student Response Book** (pages 26–33)

Instructions

Introduce the activity: **We read a story about Moe and learned why he was not happy. Sometimes Moe is happy, and sometimes Moe is sad. Wearing a crown makes Moe happy. Coming to school to see you makes me happy. Eating ice cream makes me happy. Now we are going to look at some pictures of people and decide if we think they are happy or sad.**

Open the Student Response Book and point to each picture for happy. Say, **This person is happy. And this person is happy. This person is happy, too.**

Point to a picture of someone who is happy as a model. Give each student a turn to point to a picture of someone who is happy. Say, **(Student's name), point to happy.** If the student does not point, point to a picture and repeat the direction. If needed, physically guide the student's hand, saying, **This is happy.**

Give each student a turn, pointing to a picture of someone who is happy with each turn.

Turn to the next three student pages, which have *happy* and three distractors, and say, **OK, I'm trying to trick you! Point to the picture of happy.**

Give each student a turn. Use prompts as necessary.

Turn to the next four student pages and repeat the above script with: **sad.**

End the activity by saying, **Great job! Now let's use these words to write another page in your book.**

Assisting Students

Prompt If the student does not point to the picture, physically guide his or her hand, saying, **This is happy (sad).**

Correction If the student points to the wrong picture, model pointing to the correct picture, saying, **This is happy (sad). Now you point to happy (sad).** If the student still does not point to the correct picture, physically guide his or her hand. Give a turn to another classmate, and praise that student for doing it correctly.

Objective 14

Use new vocabulary words and personal information to create a story

Activity

Fun with Writing

Materials

- "My Book About Me" books completed by students in previous lessons
- "My Book About Me, _____ makes me happy" page in Appendix D
- Pencils, crayons, rubber alphabet stamps, glue
- Pictures of objects, actions, or events that make the students happy

Tips

- If a student is not able to write, have the student ask someone to write for him or her. If the student is not verbal, program an AAC device to state, "______ makes me happy." You can also create each student's response to what makes him or her happy using a word processor and print in a size that will fit on the page. Students can also use the rubber alphabet stamps to stamp their responses.
- If the student is not able to read the sentences in their books, program an AAC device to read the sentences or to read the new sentence.
- If a student is not able to verbalize for the lesson closing, use an AAC device to say, "Goodbye, Moe."

Instructions

In this activity, students complete another page of their "My Book About Me" books by stamping their response to what makes them happy at the beginning of the first sentence, by writing their responses with your assistance, or by gluing their responses (which have been prepared) on the line.

Introduce the activity: **Remember that you started making a book that was all about you! Today you are going to add another page to your book. But first, you have to find your books.**

Lay out the "My Book About Me" books, asking students to identify their own. Review their book covers by reading the titles and pointing to the words as you read. Have each student point to their photos on the front of their books. Have students reread the pages of their books. Then present the pictures of objects, actions, and events that make them happy.

Say, **Pick a picture of something that makes you happy.**

Distribute the new "My Book About Me" page. Help them paste the chosen picture at the top of the page. Help students complete the sentence "______ makes me happy." Then help them write their responses to complete the sentence about what makes them happy, and add the page to their books. Read the sentences together.

▶ Lesson Closing

Have Moe whisper in your ear. **Boys and girls, Moe said that you are hard workers! Moe has to leave now, but he'll be back tomorrow! Say goodbye to Moe!** Have students say goodbye to Moe verbally or by using their AAC devices.

Lesson 2

Materials

- Moe the frog puppet
- Sight word flashcards: me, is, friend
- 2" × 2" Post-it® notes
- **Level 2 Student Response Book** (pages 34–61)
- Magnetic dry erase board and marker
- **All About Moe** easel book: "Moe Is Not Happy" story
- Pencils, crayons, alphabetic rubber stamps, glue
- "My Book About Me" books completed by students in previous lessons
- "My Book About Me, _____ makes me sad" page in Appendix D
- Pictures of objects, actions, and events that make the students sad

Optional Materials

- AAC device
- Pointer/light pointer
- Plexiglas® for eye gazing
- Optional pictures or text for AAC device (see Appendix H):
  - Lesson Opening: Come out, Moe
  - Objective 4: crown
  - Objective 14: ______ makes me sad.
  - Lesson Closing: Goodbye, Moe
- Moe's Crown (see Appendix I)

Tips

- If needed, use the magnetic dry erase board and a marker (or magnetic objects) for reinforcement. Draw a line on the magnet board dividing it into two columns. At the top of the first column, place a picture of the student. At the top of the second column, place a picture of yourself. When a student responds appropriately, congratulate him or her for good work and place a mark on the student side. If a student does not respond appropriately, place a mark on your side. At the end of the lesson, count the marks and find out who had more for that day. Encourage students to participate by being enthusiastic about the marks they received.
- If a student requires an augmentative or alternative communication (AAC) device, preprogram it using the text from the optional materials list.
- All student materials (including AAC overlays and the "My Book About Me" pages) can be printed from Disc 1. Printing from the disc allows you to adapt the materials for students.
- If you are working with a student whose mode of responding is to eye-gaze, the student response options can be printed from Disc 1, laminated, and cut apart. The student choices can be adhered to Plexiglas® with Velcro®. Point to the correct answer after the student gazes to it to provide the watching peers with feedback.

▶ Lesson Opening

Engage the students by saying, **Moe, where are you?** Have students call for Moe or use their AAC devices to say, "Come out, Moe." Have Moe appear.

Moe is not so happy today, and we'll find out why when we read his story. First, let's play the Flashcard Game.

Objective 1

Read sight words using time-delay instruction

Activity

Flashcard Game

Materials

- Moe the frog puppet
- Sight word flashcards: me, is, friend

Tip

A constant time-delay procedure is used to promote near-errorless responding. If a student is making errors in Round 1, which is the 0-second time-delay round, he or she may need additional practice (outside of this lesson) in imitating your model of choosing the correct response. Using pictures, have the student practice pointing where you point until he or she can do so fluently. If the student makes mistakes in Round 2, which is the 5-second time-delay round, shorten the time before you show the correct answer to 2 seconds. He or she will only have time to answer if certain. The student may also need to practice "wait training" to wait for the response. To do "wait training," use several sheets of different colored paper and say, **Point to the paper.** Have the student wait for you to point to show him or her which sheet.

Instructions

Flashcard Game: Part I. Part I of the Flashcard Game will give students practice saying or pointing to words with guidance.

Round 1: In this round, point to the correct answer as you ask the student to point (0-second time delay).

Lay the sight word flashcards in front of the students. Introduce the activity: **Let's play a game. I'll point to a word, then you point to the same word. Watch me.**

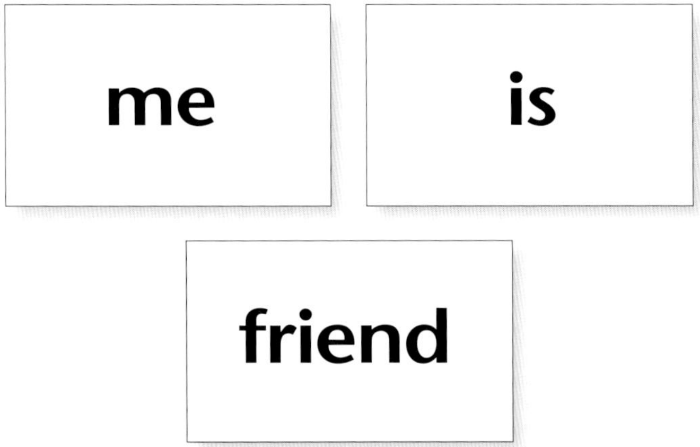

Move the sight word flashcards in front of the first student. Point to the sight word ______ while saying, **This word is ______. (Student name), now you point to ______.**

Be sure you are pointing to the sight word as you say the word. Don't move your finger until the student points to where you are pointing. If you know a student will not imitate you, guide his or her hand for correct responding. For students who eye-gaze, use a light pointer or tap the answer to get them to focus their gaze on the correct answer.

When the student points to ______, say, **Yes, ______.** For students who are verbal, also say, **What word?** and have them say the word.

Wonderful job pointing to the word ______!

Shuffle the sight word flashcards and display them in a new order in front of the next student. In this round, each student takes a

turn pointing to the same sight word before moving on to the next sight word.

(Second student's name), point to ______. Be sure you are pointing to ______ as you say the word. Use the same prompt if required.

After each student's turn, shuffle the sight words around so they are not in the same position. Repeat shuffling sight words and pointing to the words until each student has had a turn with each word. Be sure all students are watching during each student's turn to encourage incidental learning.

Round 2: In Round 2 of the Flashcard Game, students point to or say the sight word independently. Moe is ready to help after giving the student up to 5 seconds to initiate a response (a 5-second time delay).

Have Moe whisper in your ear. **Okeydokey, Moe. We can do that. Moe wants you to find the word. He can help you if you are not sure. (Student's name), find the word _____.**

Allow the student 5 seconds to point to the word. After the student finds the word, have Moe point to the same word with the student. **(Student's name), you point with Moe. Thank you for helping, Moe.**

If the student is verbal, have him or her say the word also. If the student does not point, have Moe prompt the answer and restate the word.

Give each student a turn to practice pointing to the sight word you name. Shuffle the sight words and repeat the process for each student with the remaining word. Be sure all students are watching each other's turn.

Awesome playing the Flashcard Game! Moe is learning to read and so are you! Let's play the next game!

Assisting Students

Prompt If the student does not point to the word, use Moe to point to the correct word, saying, **Moe pointed to ______. Now you point to ______.** If the student still does not point, physically guide his or her hand.

Correction If the student points to the wrong word, model the correct response by pointing to the correct word and saying, **This is the word ______. Now you point to ______.** If the student still does not point to the correct word, physically guide his or her hand. Give a turn to another classmate, and praise that student for doing it correctly.

Pile on the Praise

Objective 2

Point to the sight words to complete sentences

Activity

Flashcard Game

Materials

- Moe the frog puppet
- Sight word flashcards: me, is, friend
- **Level 2 Student Response Book** (pages 34–39)

Instructions

Flashcard Game: Part II. Display the Student Response Book. Place Moe's mouth near your ear and appear to be intently listening. **Moe wants you to read your new word in a sentence. Moe, why do you need to read the words in sentences?** Place Moe's mouth near your ear again. **I see . . . that's what the "big frogs" do! The "big frogs" read words in sentences. Then that's what we want to do!**

Model reading sentence A.1 while pointing to each word in the sentence. Place verbal emphasis on the underlined word. **He sat next to me. Listen again. He sat next to me.**

Read sentence B.1, pointing to each word. **He sat next to ______.** Point to the blank space.

Place the sight word flashcards in front of a student, using the correct answer and one distractor. **Show Moe which word goes here** (pointing back to the blank space in the sentence). **What word goes here? ______ or ______?**

Allow the student 5 seconds to respond. If the student responds correctly, affirm by saying, **Yes, me. He sat next to me.**

Shuffle the sight words and repeat the script with sentences A.2 **"The book is on the table"** and B.2, as well as sentences A.3 **"I am going to see my friend"** and B.3.

Assisting Students

Prompt If the student does not respond within 5 seconds, read sentence A again, placing verbal emphasis on the sight word. Then read sentence B, pausing at the blank space.

______ is the word that goes here. I can find ______. Point to the correct sight word and say, **(Student's name), point to ______ with me. Yes, ______.**

Correction Do not allow students to practice incorrect responses. For a student who can point and is about to point to an incorrect response, physically guide his or her hand to the correct response while verbally reinforcing the response. For students who use eye-gaze and are visually attending to the incorrect response, remove the incorrect response and visually cue them to the correct response.

Objective 3

Point to text as it is read

Activity

Pointing to Words

Materials

- Moe the frog puppet
- "Moe Is Not Happy" story
- **Level 2 Student Response Book** (page 40)

Tips

- Use a wait time of 5 seconds for all responses in this activity. However, students may need longer than 5 seconds initially. In this case, responding within 5 seconds should be viewed as a goal to work toward. Note and track response time for any student for whom you feel it is physically difficult to respond within 5 seconds.
- The goal of text pointing in this level is to have students move left-to-right and top-to-bottom.
- Do not slow your speed of reading to accommodate students' speed of movement. Work toward having students keep pace with your speed of reading as they point to the text.

Instructions

Introduce the activity by saying, **Today we are going to read "Moe Is Not Happy."**

While displaying the easel book so all can see, read "Moe Is Not Happy" with enthusiasm, pointing to the text, moving from left-to-right and top-to-bottom while you read.

After reading the story, return to the text-pointing page. Say, **Now Moe needs help reading his story. You can help him. I want you to point to each word in the line that I read. Like this.** While displaying the book so all can see, read lines 5 and 6 of "Moe Is Not Happy." Point to each word in lines 5 and 6 as you read. Then choose a student to point. Students can point to the text in the story, or you can use the page in the Student Response Book.

(Student's name), your turn! Point to the words for Moe as I read the line. I'm going to show you where to start, and I want you to follow along by pointing to each word as I read it. Show the student where to start pointing by touching the first word.

Repeat for each student, using the lines in the book (or in the Student Response Book).

Let's find out what Moe wants to do next!

Assisting Students

Prompt Modeling for the correct response is already built into the script. A student is given 5 seconds to begin responding. If the student does not initiate a response within 5 seconds, provide a visual cue. A visual cue may be tapping the page in the book and modeling the pointing. If there is still no response within 5 seconds, physically guide the student's hand to point to the words.

Objective 4

Say and/or point to a word to complete a repeated story line

Activity

Hidden Words

Materials

- Moe the frog puppet
- "Moe Is Not Happy" story (prepare for this activity by adhering a Post-it® note to cover the word *crown* highlighted in yellow in story line 9)
- **Level 2 Student Response Book** (page 41)

Tips

- For students who eye-gaze, print the student page from Disc 1 and cut the choices apart. Place the choices a distance apart so that you can discriminate the students' purposeful choices.

- If a student is not able to verbalize, program the AAC device to say the hidden word. Let the student activate the AAC device to say the hidden word and to choose the picture representing the hidden word.

Instructions

Have Moe whisper to you. **Let's play the Hidden Words game! I am going to read a line from the "Moe Is Not Happy" story, and I will point to a word that is hidden** (covered with the Post-it® note). **Get ready!**

Read line 8 from "Moe Is Not Happy," emphasizing the word *crown.*

Read line 9, pausing to remove the Post-it® note. Point to the word *crown* and say, **Crown.**

Again cover the word *crown* in line 9. Say, **It's your turn, boys and girls! I am going to read these lines, and this time I want you (or a student's name) to say the hidden word. Get ready!**

Read lines 8 and 9, pausing for a student to indicate the hidden word *crown* in line 9. Uncover the word when students say it. Repeat until all students have had a turn.

Now Moe wants you to point to the picture and the word that tells what the hidden word was. First Moe is going to show you how to do it, and then you will have a turn. I will read the lines again, and he will point to a picture that tells what the uncovered word is. He has two choices here.

Point to the pictures in the Student Response Book and tell the students what the two choices are. Read lines 8 and 9 again, pausing on line 9 for Moe to point to the picture/word representing *crown.* Encourage students to say the uncovered word (use an AAC device for nonverbal students). Repeat the sequence for each student.

Assisting Students

Prompt If there is no response within 5 seconds, provide the student with a visual cue. A visual cue might consist of tapping (or using a light pointer to point to) the correct response. Say the word as you give the visual cue. If there is still no response within 5 seconds, physically guide the student's hand to the correct response. Say the word as you give the physical cue.

Objective 5

Respond to literal questions about a story

Activity

Answering Questions

Materials

- Moe the frog puppet
- "Moe Is Not Happy" story
- **Level 2 Student Response Book** (pages 42–45)

Tips

- Each line is numbered in the story. In this activity, lines 2, 4, 7, and 10 are appropriate places to ask questions. When reading "Moe Is Not Happy," stop to ask questions at lines 2, 4, 7, and 10. You do not need to ask each student each question; rather, have students take turns answering the questions.
- For students who eye-gaze, print the student page from Disc 1 and cut the choices apart. Place the choices a distance apart so that you can discriminate the students' purposeful choices.
- Reproduce onto heavy stock paper, color, and cut out Moe's crown (see Appendix H of the **ELSB Implementation Guide**) and use as a prop during story reading.

Instructions

Start by having Moe whisper to you. **Moe wants to hear his story again. But this time, I am going to ask you some questions about Moe. You are going to answer the questions by pointing to a picture. The answers are here.** Touch the page in the Student Response Book. **Get ready!**

Read the story "Moe Is Not Happy," stopping to ask the following questions at the end of the designated lines. After asking the question, point to and name the answer choices in the Student Response Book, and then ask the question again. Encourage students who are verbal to point to the correct response and to say the correct response.

Question 1 from Line 2: **Is Moe happy every day?**
Question 2 from Line 4: **Who is sad?**
Question 3 from Line 7: **What does Moe say?**
Question 4 from Line 10: **What does Moe do?**

Assisting Students

Prompt If there is no response within 5 seconds, provide the student with a visual cue. For this skill, you might ask Moe to do the visual prompt (e.g., say, **Moe, can you help [student's name] find the answer?**). A visual cue might consist of having Moe tap the correct response. Say, **Moe has shown you the answer. Now I will read the question again, and you show me the answer.** Read the question a second time. If there is still no response within 5 seconds, physically guide the student's hand to the correct response. Say the word as you give the physical cue.

Correction Do not allow students to practice incorrect responses. For a student who can point and is about to point to an incorrect response, physically guide his or her hand to the correct response while verbally reinforcing the response. For students who use eye-gaze and are visually attending to the incorrect response, remove the incorrect response and visually cue them to the correct response.

Objective 6

Demonstrate understanding of syllable segmentation by clapping out syllables in words

Activity

Chunking Words

Materials

- Moe the frog puppet

Tip

A great deal of thought must be given to how a student who is physically challenged will demonstrate this skill. When providing physical cues, make sure the cue can be faded over time. In order for the cue to be faded, the movement you choose must be one the student can create independently (e.g., don't use clapping as a physical cue if the student is unable to clap independently). One way to determine the best movement for the student to use would be to turn on some music, demonstrate moving to the music, and then watch to see what body part the student is able to move independently.

Instructions

Place Moe's mouth near your ear and appear to be listening intently. **Moe is very shy. He says words in a funny way. He says the sounds in words very slowly. Sometimes it is hard to figure out what he means. Moe wants us to help him. He wants to say *hello*. Okeydokey, Moe, you say *hello*.** Listen with concern as Moe says the word *hello*.

Have Moe say, ***Hel...lo,*** slowly dividing it into two syllables.

Moe said *hello* the slow way. He said *hel...lo*. I think he is trying to tell us the syllables he hears in *hel...lo*. Moe, say *hello* again, and we'll clap out the syllables.

Model tapping out the two syllables in the word *hello* as Moe says the word. Make certain that Moe says the word *hello* slowly, clearly dividing the syllables as he speaks.

Have Moe say, ***Hel...lo.***

Let's say *hello* again slowly and clap out the syllables for Moe. I'll clap and you help me. *Hel...lo*. Help me do that again, boys and girls. Repeat the script.

Have Moe whisper in your ear. **Moe wants to try again with more words. Moe, you choose the next word!**

Have Moe say, **(student's name).**

Repeat the above script using **a student's name, *jumping*,** and **other students' names** that are two to three syllables in length.

Objective 8

Identify letter-sound correspondences

Activity

Letter Sounds Game

Materials

- Moe the frog puppet
- **Level 2 Student Response Book** (pages 46–48)

Tip

When a letter appears between two virgules (/ /), say the sound the letter makes rather than the letter name (e. g., /a/ means to make the *a* sound). Stretch the sound when multiple letters (e.g., /aaa/) appear within the virgules.

Instructions

Letter Sounds Game: Part I. Part I reviews the letter *a* and the sound short *a* makes. Introduce the activity: **We are going to play the Letter Sounds Game. It's a fun game. Here we go.**

Touch below the *a* on the Sound Presentation page in the Student Response Book and say, **This letter *a* says /aaa/. Touch /aaa/ with me.** Be sure you are pointing below the *a* as you say the sound. Don't move your finger until the student points to where you are pointing. **Your turn. Touch /aaa/.** Give each student an opportunity to touch the *a*.

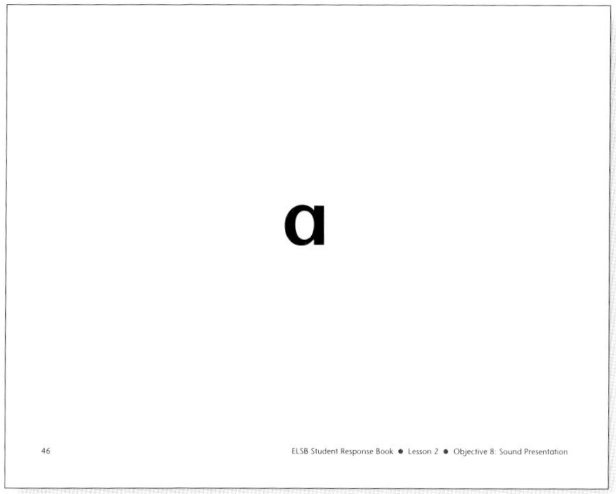
a

46 ELSB Student Response Book • Lesson 2 • Objective 8: Sound Presentation

Letter Sounds Game: Part II. Part II helps students discriminate the short *a* sound from one distractor. Introduce the activity: **Now we get to do the next page of the Letter Sounds Game. Get ready!**

Turn to the Letter-Sound Discrimination page in the Student Response Book. **Touch /aaa/. Good job touching /aaa/. The letter *a* says /aaa/.** Give each student an opportunity to touch the *a*.

Whether students are verbal or nonverbal, encourage them to make the sound for short *a*. **This time I will touch the *a* and you say the sound /aaa/. Ready?** Give each student an opportunity to say /a/.

For review, repeat the above script for the ***m*** sound.

Letter Sounds Game: Part III. Part III helps students identify and discriminate the short *a* sound when it is the beginning sound in words.

Turn to the Aggie and Ally page in the Student Response Book and say, **Our special sound is /aaa/. Let's practice. Touch /aaa/. Nice touching /aaa/. We are going to play a really fun game.**

First, we will listen to a poem about Aggie and Ally. Aggie and Ally are alligators, and they love words that start with /aaa/. Let's read their poem and see if we can hear words that start with /aaa/.

Read the following poem one time. While you read, point to the *a* on the Aggie and Ally page each time you say a word that begins with short *a*.

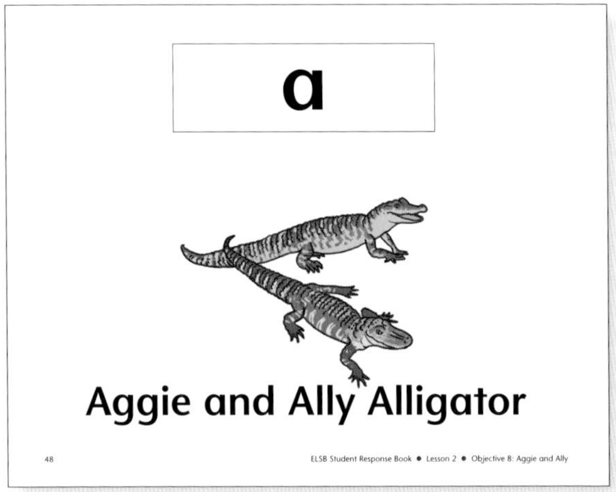

Aggie and Ally

Aggie the **a**lligator lives down in the bay
With her sister named **A**lly on
"**A**lligator Way."
Aggie **a**nd **A**lly work in the morning
And play in the **a**fternoon.
They play a game called "**A**fternoon Moon."
They swim up in the water **a**nd go snap, snap, snap.
They swim down in the water **a**nd go whap, whap, whap!
Then **A**ggie **A**lligator **a**nd **A**lly **A**lligator
Take a long, long **a**fternoon nap!

I will read the poem again and point to /aaa/ when I hear words that begin with /aaa/. This time you help me. You touch /aaa/ when you hear a word that starts with /aaa/.

Read the poem a second time and encourage students to listen and point to the *a* on the Aggie and Ally page when they hear words that begin with /a/. Stretch the beginning sound to emphasize the *a*. When a student touches the *a* at the appropriate time, give feedback and praise. For example: **Good. The first sound in *alligator* is /aaa/.** Note that students may find it difficult to point to the sound every time they hear it, but even pointing to the sound some of the time helps develop their phonemic awareness.

Assisting Students

Prompt If you know a student will not imitate you, guide his or her hand for correct responding. For students who eye-gaze, use a light pointer or tap the answer to get them to focus their gaze on the correct answer.

Correction Touch below the *a* and say, **This sound is /aaa/. Say /aaa/ with me. /aaa/. Say it by yourself. What sound?**

Objective 9

Point to and/or say the first/last sounds in words

Activity

First/Last Sound Game

Materials

- Moe the frog puppet
- **Level 2 Student Response Book** (page 49)

Tips

- When you say the word the "fast way," touch the colored smiley face to focus students, say "Ready," then slash under the word as you say it.
- Stretch the sound when multiple letters appear in the virgules (e.g., /mmm/). Note that some sounds cannot be stretched (e.g., /t/).

Instructions

Place Moe's mouth near your ear and appear to be listening. **Moe wants us to get really good at knowing the first sounds in words. Moe has a fun game to play with colored smiling faces to help us hear the first sounds in words. Okeydokey, Moe! We are ready to play the First/Last Sound Game.**

Touch the green smiley face on the student page. **Get ready to read the word that comes after the green smiley face. I'll touch and say the first sound /mmm/. Then I will touch and say the next sound /aaa/. Then I will touch and say the last sound /t/. Say the sounds in this word with me /mmm/ /aaa/ /t/.**

I can say this word the fast way. Ready (put your finger on the smiley face, then say the word *mat* without segmenting it into sounds), ***mat*. Say this word the fast way with me, *mat*. Yes, *mat*. We said *mat* the fast way.**

Touch the first sound in *mat*. **The first sound in *mat* is /mmm/. Touch the first sound in *mat*.**

Say the first sound in *mat*. Place emphasis on the beginning sound when you say the word *mat*. **Yes, /mmm/ is the first sound in the word *mat*.**

Repeat the script above for: **at, as, man,** changing the script to match the color of the smiley face and the beginning sound you are focusing on.

Assisting Students

Prompt If you know a student will not imitate you, guide his or her hand for correct responding. For students who eye-gaze, use a light pointer or tap the answer to get them to focus their gaze on the correct answer.

Correction Touch below each sound and say, **This sound is /___/. Say /___/ with me. /___/. Say it by yourself. What sound?**

Objective 10

Identify pictures that begin/end with given sounds

Activity

Finding Pictures with Special Sounds

Materials

- Moe the frog puppet
- **Level 2 Student Response Book** (pages 50–53)

Instructions

Place Moe's mouth near your ear and appear to be listening. **Moe is ready to play his game Finding Pictures with Special Sounds. The special sounds today are /mmm/ and /aaa/.**

Display the Student Response Book. Point to each picture as you name it (fish, add, nurse, leaf), placing emphasis on the first sound in each word.

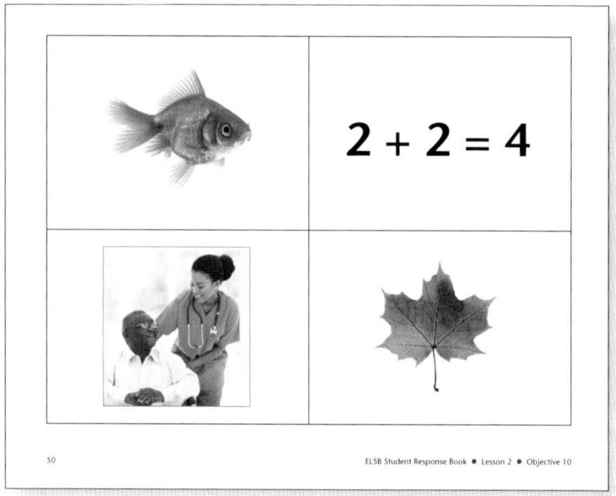

Say the picture words with me. The first sound in *fish* is /fff/. The first sound in *add* is /aaa/. The first sound in *nurse* is /nnn/. The first sound in *leaf* is /lll/.

Point to the picture that has /aaa/ as its first sound. Show me the picture that starts with /aaa/.

Have a student point to add. **Yes, the first sound in the word *add* is /aaa/.**

Repeat the above script for each student page. Change the script to match the target sound. The target response (focusing on either /a/ or /m/) has an asterisk in the list below.

fork, fan, nut, *man
ball, foot, *ant, pie
***mail, soup, sun, dog**

Give all students 5 seconds to respond after you say, **Show me the picture that starts with ______.**

Assisting Students

Prompt and Correction

If there is no response within 5 seconds, point to the correct response and say, **The first sound in _____ is /___/. Touch the picture of _____.** If the student does not respond within 5 seconds, physically guide the student's hand to the correct response and say, ___ **starts with /___/.**

Objective 13

Point to pictures/words representing new vocabulary

Activity

The New Word Game

Materials

- Moe the frog puppet
- **Level 2 Student Response Book** (pages 54–61)

Instructions

Introduce the activity: **We read a story about Moe and learned why he was not happy. Sometimes Moe is happy, and sometimes Moe is sad. Wearing a crown makes Moe happy. Coming to school to see you makes me happy. Eating ice cream makes me happy. Now we are going to look at some pictures of people and decide if we think they are happy or sad. When someone gets hurt, I am sad. This person is sad, too.**

Open the Student Response Book and point to each picture for sad. Say, **This person is sad. And this person is sad. This person is sad, too.**

Give each student a turn to point to a picture of someone who is sad. Say, **(Student's name), point to sad.** If the student does not point, point to a picture and repeat the direction. If needed, physically guide the student's hand, saying, **This is sad.**

Give each student a turn, pointing to a picture of someone who is sad with each turn.

Turn to the next three student pages, which have *sad* and three distractors, and say, **OK, I'm trying to trick you! Point to the picture of sad.**

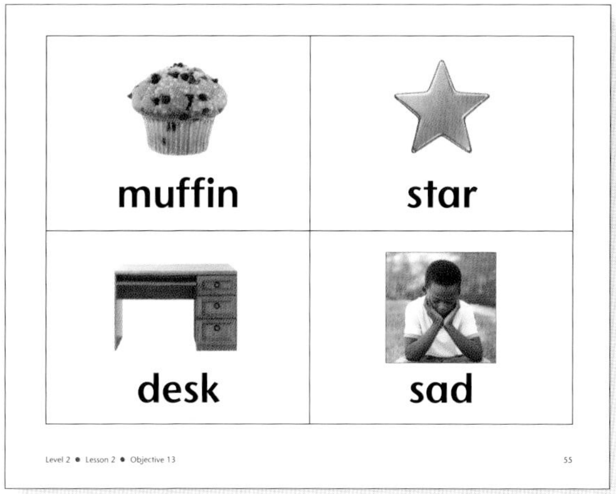

Give each student a turn. Use prompts as necessary.

Turn to the next four student pages and repeat the above script with: **happy.**

End the activity by saying, **Great job! Now let's use these words to write another page in your books about you.**

Assisting Students

Prompt If the student does not point to the picture, physically guide his or her hand, saying, **This is sad (happy).**

Correction If the student points to the wrong picture, model pointing to the correct picture, saying, **This is sad (happy). Now you point to sad (happy).** If the student still does not point to the correct picture, physically guide his or her hand. Give a turn to another classmate, and praise that student for doing it correctly.

Objective 14

Use new vocabulary words and personal information to create a story

Activity

Fun with Writing

Materials

- "My Book About Me" books completed by students in previous lessons
- "My Book About Me, _____ makes me sad" page in Appendix D
- Pencils, crayons, rubber alphabet stamps, glue
- Pictures of objects, actions, or events that make the students sad

Tips

- If a student is not able to write, have the student ask someone to write for him or her. If the student is not verbal, program an AAC device to state, "______ makes me sad." You can also create each student's response to what makes him or her sad using a word processor and print in a size that will fit on the page. Students can also use the rubber alphabet stamps to stamp their responses.
- If the student is not able to read the sentences in their books, program an AAC device to read the sentences or to read the new sentence.
- If a student is not able to verbalize for the lesson closing, use an AAC device to say, "Goodbye, Moe."

Instructions

In this activity, students complete another page of their "My Book About Me" books by stamping their response to what makes them sad at the beginning of the first sentence, by writing their responses with your assistance, or by gluing their responses (which have been prepared) on the line.

Introduce the activity: **Remember that you started making a book that was all about you! Today you are going to add another page to your book. But first, you have to find your books.**

Lay out the "My Book About Me" books, asking students to identify their own. Review their book covers by reading the titles and pointing to the words as you read. Have each student point to their photos on the front of their books. Have students reread the pages of their books. Then present the pictures of objects, actions, and events that make them sad.

Say, **Pick a picture of something that makes you sad.**

Distribute the new "My Book About Me" page. Help them glue the chosen picture at the top of the page. Help students complete the sentence "______ makes me sad." Then help them write their responses to complete the sentence about what makes them sad, and add the page to their books. Read the sentences together.

Lesson Closing

Have Moe whisper in your ear. **Boys and girls, Moe said that you are learning so much! Moe has to leave now, but he'll be back tomorrow! Say goodbye to Moe!** Have students say goodbye to Moe verbally or by using their AAC devices.

Lesson 3

Materials

- Moe the frog puppet
- Sight word flashcards: me, is, friend
- 2" × 2" Post-it® notes
- **Level 2 Student Response Book** (pages 62–89)
- Magnetic dry erase board and marker
- **All About Moe** easel book: "Moe Is Happy" story
- "My Book About Me" books completed by students in previous lessons
- "My Book About Me, _____ makes me mad" page in Appendix D
- Pencils, crayons, alphabetic rubber stamps, glue
- Pictures of objects, actions, and events that make the students mad

Optional Materials

- AAC device
- Pointer/light pointer
- Plexiglas® for eye gazing
- Optional pictures or text for AAC device (see Appendix H):
  - Lesson Opening: Come here, Moe
  - Objective 4: frog
  - Objective 14: ______ makes me mad.
  - Lesson Closing: Goodbye, Moe

Tips

- If needed, use the magnetic dry erase board and a marker (or magnetic objects) for reinforcement. Draw a line on the magnet board dividing it into two columns. At the top of the first column, place a picture of the student. At the top of the second column, place a picture of yourself. When a student responds appropriately, congratulate him or her for good work and place a mark on the student side. If a student does not respond appropriately, place a mark on your side. At the end of the lesson, count the marks and find out who had more for that day. Encourage students to participate by being enthusiastic about the marks they received.

- If a student requires an augmentative or alternative communication (AAC) device, preprogram it using the text from the optional materials list.

- All student materials (including AAC overlays and the "My Book About Me" pages) can be printed from Disc 1. Printing from the disc allows you to adapt the materials for students.

- If you are working with a student whose mode of responding is to eye-gaze, the student response options can be printed from Disc 1, laminated, and cut apart. The student choices can be adhered to Plexiglas® with Velcro®. Point to the correct answer after the student gazes to it to provide the watching peers with feedback.

▶ Lesson Opening

Engage the students by welcoming Moe to the class. Say, **Let's call Moe out this morning! Come here, Moe!** Have students call Moe or use their AAC devices to call Moe. Have Moe hop out from under the table and sit on your shoulder. Have Moe whisper to you. **Oh, Moe, I'm so excited for you! Moe is happy today! I think that his new story will tell us why he's so happy! First, let's play our Flashcard Game, and then we will read the new story!**

Objective 1

Read sight words using time-delay instruction

Activity

Flashcard Game

Materials

- Moe the frog puppet
- Sight word flashcards: me, is, friend

Tip

A constant time-delay procedure is used to promote near-errorless responding. If a student is making errors in Round 1, which is the 0-second time-delay round, he or she may need additional practice (outside of this lesson) in imitating your model of choosing the correct response. Using pictures, have the student practice pointing where you point until he or she can do so fluently. If the student makes mistakes in Round 2, which is the 5-second time-delay round, shorten the time before you show the correct answer to 2 seconds. He or she will only have time to answer if certain. The student may also need to practice "wait training" to wait for the response. To do "wait training," use several sheets of different colored paper and say, **Point to the paper.** Have the student wait for you to point to show him or her which sheet.

Instructions

Flashcard Game: Part I. Part I of the Flashcard Game will give students practice saying or pointing to words with guidance.

Round 1: In this round, point to the correct answer as you ask the student to point (0-second time delay).

Lay the sight word flashcards in front of the students. Introduce the activity: **Let's play a game. I'll point to a word, then you point to the same word. Watch me.**

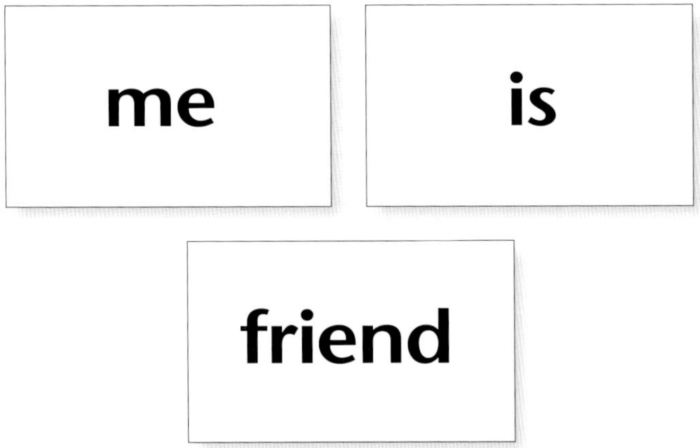

Move the sight word flashcards in front of the first student. Point to the sight word ______ while saying, **This word is ______. (Student name), now you point to ______.**

Be sure you are pointing to the sight word as you say the word. Don't move your finger until the student points to where you are pointing. If you know a student will not imitate you, guide his or her hand for correct responding. For students who eye-gaze, use a light pointer or tap the answer to get them to focus their gaze on the correct answer.

When the student points to ______, say, **Yes, ______.** For students who are verbal, also say, **What word?** and have them say the word.

Wonderful job pointing to the word ______!

Shuffle the sight word flashcards and display them in a new order in front of the next student. In this round, each student takes a turn pointing to the same sight word before moving on to the next sight word.

(Second student's name), point to ______. Be sure you are pointing to ______ as you say the word. Use the same prompt if required.

After each student's turn, shuffle the sight words around so they are not in the same position. Repeat shuffling sight words and pointing to the words until each student has had a turn with each word. Be sure all students are watching during each student's turn to encourage incidental learning.

Round 2: In Round 2 of the Flashcard Game, students point to or say the sight word independently. Moe is ready to help after giving the student up to 5 seconds to initiate a response (a 5-second time delay).

Have Moe whisper in your ear. **Okeydokey, Moe. We can do that. Moe wants you to find the word. He can help you if you are not sure. (Student's name), find the word ______.**

Allow the student 5 seconds to point to the word. After the student finds the word, have Moe point to the same word with the student. **(Student's name), you point with Moe. Thank you for helping, Moe.**

If the student is verbal, have him or her say the word also. If the student does not point, have Moe prompt the answer and restate the word.

Give each student a turn to practice pointing to the sight word you name. Shuffle the sight words and repeat the process for each student with the remaining words. Be sure all students are watching each other's turn.

Awesome playing the Flashcard Game! Moe is learning to read and so are you!

Assisting Students

Prompt If the student does not point to the word, use Moe to point to the correct word, saying, **Moe pointed to ______. Now you point to ______.** If the student still does not point, physically guide his or her hand.

Correction If the student points to the wrong word, model the correct response by pointing to the correct word and saying, **This is the word ______. Now you point to ______.** If the student still does not point to the correct word, physically guide his or her hand. Give a turn to another classmate, and praise that student for doing it correctly.

Objective 2

Point to the sight words to complete sentences

Activity

Flashcard Game

Materials

- Moe the frog puppet
- Sight word flashcards: me, is, friend
- **Level 2 Student Response Book** (pages 62–67)

Instructions

Flashcard Game: Part II. Display the Student Response Book. Place Moe's mouth near your ear and appear to be intently listening. **Moe wants you to read your new word in a sentence. Moe, why do you need to read the words in sentences?** Place Moe's mouth near your ear again. **I see . . . that's what the "big frogs" do! The "big frogs" read words in sentences. Then that's what we want to do!**

Model reading sentence A.1 while pointing to each word in the sentence. Place verbal emphasis on the underlined word. **Give the ball to me, please. Listen again. Give the ball to me, please.**

Read sentence B.1, pointing to each word. **Give the ball to ______, please.** Point to the blank space.

Place the sight word flashcards in front of a student, using the correct answer and one distractor. **Show Moe which word goes here** (pointing back to the blank space in the sentence). **What word goes here? ______ or ______?**

Allow the student 5 seconds to respond. If the student responds correctly, affirm by saying, **Yes, me. Give the ball to me, please.**

Shuffle the sight words and repeat the script with sentences A.2 "**Where is my hat?**" and B.2, as well as sentences A.3 "**Kevin has a new friend**" and B.3.

Assisting Students

Prompt If the student does not respond within 5 seconds, read sentence A again, placing verbal emphasis on the sight word. Then read sentence B, pausing at the blank space.

______ is the word that goes here. I can find ______. Point to the correct sight word and say, **(Student's name), point to ______ with me. Yes, ______.**

Correction Do not allow students to practice incorrect responses. For a student who can point and is about to point to an incorrect response, physically guide his or her hand to the correct response while verbally reinforcing the response. For students who use eye-gaze and are visually attending to the incorrect response, remove the incorrect response and visually cue them to the correct response.

Objective 3

Point to text as it is read

Activity

Pointing to Words

Materials

- Moe the frog puppet
- "Moe Is Happy" story
- **Level 2 Student Response Book** (page 68)

Tips

- Use a wait time of 5 seconds for all responses in this activity. However, students may need longer than 5 seconds initially. In this case, responding within 5 seconds should be viewed as a goal to work toward. Note and track response time for any student for whom you feel it is physically difficult to respond within 5 seconds.
- The goal of text pointing in this level is to have students move left-to-right and top-to-bottom.
- Do not slow your speed of reading to accommodate students' speed of movement. Work toward having students keep pace with your speed of reading as they point to the text.

Instructions

Introduce the activity by saying, **Today we are going to read a new story, "Moe Is Happy."**

While displaying the easel book so all can see, read "Moe Is Happy" with enthusiasm, pointing to the text, moving left-to-right and top-to-bottom while you read.

After reading the story, return to the text-pointing page. Say, **Now Moe needs help reading his story. You can help him. I want you to point to each word in the line that I read. Like this.** While displaying the book so all can see, read lines 1, 2, and 3 of "Moe Is Happy." Point to each word in lines 1, 2, and 3 as you read. Then choose a student to point. Students can point to the text in the story, or you can use the page in the Student Response Book.

(Student's name), your turn! Point to the words for Moe as I read the line. I'm going to show you where to start, and I want you to follow along by pointing to each word as I read it. Show the student where to start pointing by touching the first word.

Repeat for each student, using the lines in the book (or in the Student Response Book).

Let's find out what Moe wants to do next!

Assisting Students

Prompt Modeling for the correct response is already built into the script. A student is given 5 seconds to begin responding. If the student does not initiate a response within 5 seconds, provide a visual cue. A visual cue may be tapping the page in the book and modeling the pointing. If there is still no response within 5 seconds, physically guide the student's hand to point to the words.

Objective 4

Say and/or point to a word to complete a repeated story line

Activity

Hidden Words

Materials

- Moe the frog puppet
- "Moe Is Happy" story (prepare for this activity by adhering a Post-it® note to cover the word *frog* highlighted in yellow in story line 3)
- **Level 2 Student Response Book** (page 69)

Tips

- For students who eye-gaze, print the student page from Disc 1 and cut the choices apart. Place the choices a distance apart so that you can discriminate the students' purposeful choices.
- If a student is not able to verbalize, program the AAC device to say the hidden word. Let the student activate the AAC device to say the hidden word and to choose the picture representing the hidden word.

Instructions

Have Moe whisper to you. **Let's play the Hidden Words game! I am going to read a line from the "Moe Is Happy" story, and I will point to a word that is hidden** (covered with the Post-it® note). **Get ready!**

Read lines 1 and 2 from "Moe Is Happy," emphasizing the word *frog* in line 2.

Read line 3, pausing to remove the Post-it® note. Point to the word *frog* and say, **Frog.**

Again cover the word *frog* in line 2. Say, **It's your turn, boys and girls! I am going to read these lines, and this time I want you (or a student's name) to say the hidden word. Get ready!**

Read lines 1–3, pausing for a student to indicate the hidden word *frog* in line 3. Uncover the word when students say it. Repeat until all students have had a turn.

Now Moe wants you to point to the picture and the word that tells what the hidden word was. First Moe is going to show you how to do it, and then you will have a turn. I will read the lines again, and he will point to a picture that tells what the uncovered word is. He has two choices here.

Point to the pictures in the Student Response Book and tell the students what the two choices are. Read lines 1–3, pausing on line 3 for Moe to point to the picture/word representing *frog.* Encourage students to say the uncovered word (use an AAC device for nonverbal students). Repeat the sequence for each student.

Assisting Students

Prompt If there is no response within 5 seconds, provide the student with a visual cue. A visual cue might consist of tapping (or using a light pointer to point to) the correct response. Say the word as you give the visual cue. If there is still no response within 5 seconds, physically guide the student's hand to the correct response. Say the word as you give the physical cue.

Objective 5

Respond to literal questions about a story

Activity

Answering Questions

Materials

- Moe the frog puppet
- "Moe Is Happy" story
- **Level 2 Student Response Book** (pages 70–73)

Tips

- Each line is numbered in the story. In this activity, lines 4, 6, 7, and 10 are appropriate places to ask questions. When reading "Moe Is Happy," stop to ask questions at lines 4, 6, 7, and 10. You do not need to ask each student each question; rather, have students take turns answering the questions.
- For students who eye-gaze, print the student page from Disc 1 and cut the choices apart. Place the choices a distance apart so that you can discriminate the students' purposeful choices.

Instructions

Start by having Moe whisper to you. **Moe wants to hear his story again. But this time, I am going to ask you some questions about Moe. You are going to answer the questions by pointing to a picture. The answers are here.** Touch the page in the Student Response Book. **Get ready!**

Read the story "Moe Is Happy," stopping to ask the following questions at the end of the designated lines. After asking the question, point to and name the answer choices in the Student Response Book, and then ask the question again. Encourage students who are verbal to point to the correct response and to say the correct response.

Question 1 from Line 4: **Is Moe sad today?**
Question 2 from Line 6: **Who came to play?**
Question 3 from Line 7: **Who sings?**
Question 4 from Line 10: **Who is happy?**

Assisting Students

Prompt If there is no response within 5 seconds, provide the student with a visual cue. For this skill, you might ask Moe to do the visual prompt (e.g., say, **Moe, can you help [student's name] find the answer?**). A visual cue might consist of having Moe tap the correct response. Say, **Moe has shown you the answer. Now I will read the question again, and you show me the answer.** Read the question a second time. If there is still no response within 5 seconds, physically guide the student's hand to the correct response. Say the word as you give the physical cue.

Correction Do not allow students to practice incorrect responses. For a student who can point and is about to point to an incorrect response, physically guide his or her hand to the correct response while verbally reinforcing the response. For students who use eye-gaze and are visually attending to the incorrect response, remove the incorrect response and visually cue them to the correct response.

Objective 6

Demonstrate understanding of syllable segmentation in words by clapping out syllables in words

Activity

Chunking Words

Materials

- Moe the frog puppet

Tip

A great deal of thought must be given to how a student who is physically challenged will demonstrate this skill. When providing physical cues, make sure the cue can be faded over time. In order for the cue to be faded, the movement you choose must be one the student can create independently (e.g., don't use clapping as a physical cue if the student is unable to clap independently). One way to determine the best movement for the student to use would be to turn on some music, demonstrate moving to the music, and then watch to see what body part the student is able to move independently.

Instructions

Place Moe's mouth near your ear and appear to be listening intently. **Moe is very shy. He says words in a funny way. He says the sounds in words very slowly. Sometimes it is hard to figure out what he means. Moe wants us to help him. He wants to say hello to Molly. Okeydokey, Moe, you say *Molly*.** Listen with concern as Moe says the word *Molly*.

Have Moe say, ***Mo...lly,*** slowly dividing it into two syllables.

Moe said *Molly* the slow way. He said *Mo...lly*. I think he is trying to tell us the syllables he hears in *Mo...lly*. Moe, say *Molly* again and we'll clap out the syllables.

Model clapping out the two syllables in the word *Molly* as Moe says the name. Make certain that Moe says the word *Molly* slowly, clearly dividing the syllables as he speaks.

Have Moe say, ***Mo...lly.***

Let's say *Molly* again slowly and clap out the syllables for Moe. I'll clap and you help me. *Mo...lly*. Help me do that again, boys and girls. Repeat the script.

Have Moe whisper in your ear. **Moe wants to try again with more words. Moe, you choose the next word!**

Have Moe say, ***Ha...ppy.***

Repeat the above script using ***happy*** and ***jumping.***

Objective 8

Identify letter-sound correspondences

Activity

Letter Sounds Game

Materials

- Moe the frog puppet
- **Level 2 Student Response Book** (pages 74–76)

Tip

When a letter appears between two virgules (/ /), say the sound the letter makes rather than the letter name (e.g., /s/ means to make the *s* sound). Stretch the sound when multiple letters (e.g., /sss/) appear within the virgules.

Instructions

Letter Sounds Game (Part I). Part I introduces the letter *s* and the sound *s* makes. Introduce the activity: **We are going to play the Letter Sounds Game. It's a fun game. And today we have a new sound. Get ready!**

Touch below the *s* on the Sound Presentation page in the Student Response Book and say, **The letter says /sss/. The letter *s* says /sss/. Touch /sss/ with me.** Be sure you are pointing below the *s* as you say the sound. Don't move your finger until the student points to where you are pointing. **Your turn. Touch /sss/.** Give each student an opportunity to touch the *s*.

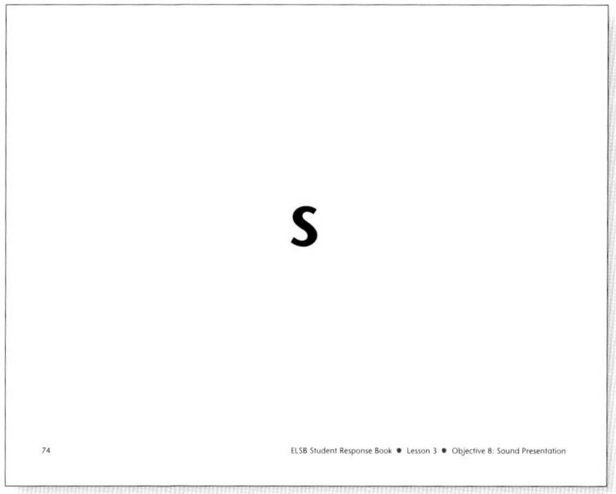

s

74 ELSB Student Response Book • Lesson 3 • Objective 8: Sound Presentation

Letter Sounds Game: Part II. Part II helps students discriminate the *s* sound from two distractors. Introduce the activity: **Now we get to do the next page of the Letter Sounds Game. Get ready!**

Turn to the Letter-Sound Discrimination page in the Student Response Book. **Touch /sss/. Good job touching /sss/. The letter *s* says /sss/.** Give each student an opportunity to touch the *s*.

Whether students are verbal or nonverbal, encourage them to make the sound for *s*. **This time I will touch the *s* and you say the sound /sss/. Ready?** Give each student an opportunity to say /s/.

For review, repeat the above script for the **short *a*** and ***m*** sounds.

Letter Sounds Game: Part III. Part III helps students identify and discriminate *s* when it is the beginning sound in words.

Turn to the Sam Seal page in the Student Response Book and say, **Our special sound is /sss/. Let's practice. Touch /sss/. Nice touching /sss/. We are going to play a really fun game. First,**

we will listen to a poem about Sam Seal. Sam Seal swims in the sea and then sits on the sand. Let's read the poem about Sam and see if we can hear words that start with /sss/.

Read the following poem one time. While you read, point to the *s* on the Sam Seal page each time you say a word that begins with *s*.

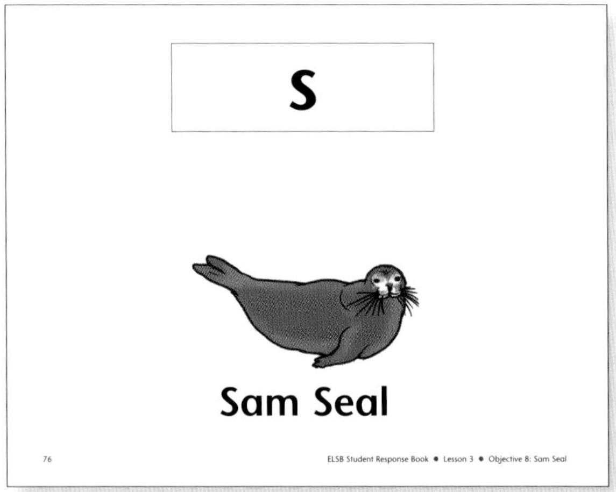

Sam Seal

Sam **S**eal lives in the **s**ea, and
Sam **S**eal lives on the land.
Sam **s**wims with flippers to move in the **s**ea,
Then **s**its in the **s**un and rests on the **s**and.
Sitting on the **s**and and **s**wimming in the **s**ea,
Sam **S**eal is **s**omewhat like you . . . and **s**omewhat like me!

I will read the poem again and point to /sss/ when I hear words that begin with /sss/. This time you help me. You touch /sss/ when you hear a word that starts with /sss/.

Read the poem a second time and encourage students to listen and point to the *s* on the Sam Seal page when they hear words that begin with /s/. Stretch the beginning sound to emphasize the *s*. When a student touches the *s* at the appropriate time, give feedback and praise. For example: **Good. The first sound in Sam is /sss/.** Note that students may find it difficult to point to the sound every time they hear it, but even pointing to the sound some of the time helps develop their phonemic awareness.

Assisting Students

Prompt If you know a student will not imitate you, guide his or her hand for correct responding. For students who eye-gaze, use a light pointer or tap the answer to get them to focus their gaze on the correct answer.

Correction Touch below the *s* and say, **This sound is /sss/. Say /sss/ with me. /sss/. Say it by yourself. What sound?**

Objective 9

Point to and/or say the first/last sounds in words

Activity

First/Last Sound Game

Materials

- Moe the frog puppet
- **Level 2 Student Response Book** (page 77)

Tips

- When you say the word the "fast way," touch the colored smiley face to focus students, say "Ready," then slash under the word as you say it.
- Stretch the sound when multiple letters appear in the virgules (e.g., /sss/). Note that some sounds cannot be stretched (e.g., /t/).

Instructions

Place Moe's mouth near your ear and appear to be listening. **Moe wants us to get really good at knowing the first sounds in words. Moe has a fun game to play with colored smiling faces to help us hear the first sounds in words. Okeydokey, Moe! We are ready to play the First/Last Sound Game.**

Touch the green smiley face on the student page. **Get ready to read the word that comes after the green smiley face. I'll touch and say the first sound /sss/. Then I will touch and say the next sound /aaa/. Then I will touch and say the last sound /t/. Say the sounds in this word with me /sss/ /aaa/ /t/.**

I can say this word the fast way. Ready (put your finger on the smiley face, then say *sat* without segmenting it into sounds), ***sat*. Say this word the fast way with me, *sat*. Yes, *sat*. We said *sat* the fast way.**

Touch the first sound in *sat*. Say, **The first sound in *sat*** is /sss/. **Touch the first sound in *sat*.** Have a student point to the *s*.

Say the first sound in *sat*. Place emphasis on the beginning sound when you say the word *sat*. **Yes, /sss/ is the first sound in the word *sat*.**

Repeat the script above for: **mat, sam, am,** changing the script to match the color of the smiley face and the beginning sound you are focusing on.

Assisting Students

Prompt If you know a student will not imitate you, guide his or her hand for correct responding. For students who eye-gaze, use a light pointer or tap the answer to get them to focus their gaze on the correct answer.

Correction Touch below each sound and say, **This sound is /___/. Say /___/ with me. /___/. Say it by yourself. What sound?**

Objective 10

Identify pictures that begin/end with given sounds

Activity

Finding Pictures with Special Sounds

Materials

- Moe the frog puppet
- **Level 2 Student Response Book** (pages 78–81)

Instructions

Place Moe's mouth near your ear and appear to be listening. **Moe is ready to play his game Finding Pictures with Special Sounds. The special sounds today are /sss/, /mmm/, and /aaa/.**

Display the Student Response Book. Point to each picture as you name it (paint, kite, sick, peas), placing emphasis on the first sound in each word.

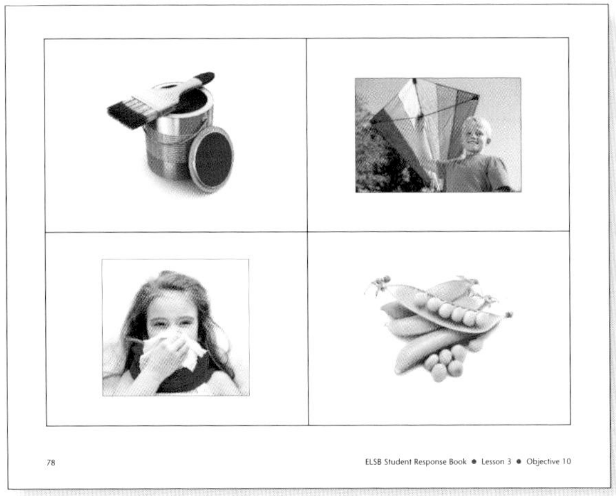

Say the picture words with me. The first sound in *paint* is /p/. The first sound in *kite* is /k/. The first sound in *sick* is /sss/. The first sound in *peas* is /p/.

Point to the picture that has /sss/ as its first sound. Show me the picture that starts with /sss/.

Have a student point to sick. **Yes, the first sound in the word *sick* is /sss/.**

Repeat the above script for each student page. Change the script to match the target sound. The target response (focusing on either /a/, /m/, or /s/) has an asterisk in the list below.

***alligator, sink, mop, rat**
lamp, cake, tooth, *milk
park, *soup, fan, apple

Give all students 5 seconds to respond after you say, **Show me the picture that starts with _____.**

Assisting Students

Prompt and Correction

If there is no response within 5 seconds, point to the correct response and say, **The first sound in ______ is /___/. Touch the picture of ______.** If the student does not respond within 5 seconds, physically guide the student's hand to the correct response and say, ______ **starts with /___/.**

Objective 13

Point to pictures/words representing new vocabulary

Activity

The New Word Game

Materials

- Moe the frog puppet
- **Level 2 Student Response Book** (pages 82–89)

Instructions

Introduce the activity: **We read a story about Moe and learned why he was happy. Sometimes Moe is happy, and sometimes Moe is sad, and sometimes Moe gets really mad! Sometimes I get mad, too. If people are mean to my students, I get mad. Coming to school to see all of you makes me happy, though. Eating ice cream makes me happy. Now we are going to look at some pictures of people and decide if we think they are happy or mad.**

Open the Student Response Book and point to each picture for mad. Say, **This person is mad. And, this person is mad. This person is mad, too.**

Give each student a turn to point to a picture of someone who is mad. Say, **(Student's name), point to mad.** If the student does not point, point to a picture and repeat the direction. If needed, physically guide the student's hand, saying, **This is mad.**

Give each student a turn, pointing to a picture of someone who is mad with each turn.

Turn to the next three student pages, which have *mad* and three distractors, and say, **OK, I'm trying to trick you! Point to the picture of mad.**

Give each student a turn. Use prompts as necessary.

Turn to the next four student pages and repeat the above script with: **happy.**

End the activity by saying, **Great job! Now let's use these words to write another page in your books about you.**

Assisting Students

Prompt If the student does not point to the picture, physically guide his or her hand, saying, **This is mad (happy).**

Correction If the student points to the wrong picture, model pointing to the correct picture, saying, **This is mad (happy). Now you point to mad (happy).** If the student still does not point to the correct picture, physically guide his or her hand. Give a turn to another classmate, and praise that student for doing it correctly.

Objective 14

Use new vocabulary words and personal information to create a story

Activity

Fun with Writing

Materials

- "My Book About Me" books completed by students in previous lessons
- "My Book About Me, _____ makes me mad" page Appendix D
- Pencils, crayons, rubber alphabet stamps, glue
- Pictures of objects, actions, or events that make the students mad

Tips

- If a student is not able to write, have the student ask someone to write for him or her. If the student is not verbal, program an AAC device to state, "_____ makes me mad." You can also create each student's response to what makes him or her mad using a word processor and print in a size that will fit on the page. Students can also use the rubber alphabet stamps to stamp their responses.
- If the student is not able to read the sentences in their books, program an AAC device to read the sentences or to read the new sentence.
- If a student is not able to verbalize for the lesson closing, use an AAC device to say, "Goodbye, Moe."

Instructions

In this activity, students complete another page of their "My Book About Me" books by stamping their response to what makes them mad at the beginning of the first sentence, by writing their responses with your assistance, or by gluing their responses (which have been prepared) on the line. Introduce the activity: **Remember that you started making a book that was all about you! Today you are going to add another page to your book. But first, you have to find your books.**

Lay out the "My Book About Me" books, asking students to identify their own. Review their book covers by reading the titles and pointing to the words as you read. Have each student point to their photos on the front of their books. Have students reread the pages of their books. Then present the pictures of objects, actions, and events that make them mad.

Say, **Pick a picture of something that makes you mad.**

Distribute the new "My Book About Me" page. Help them glue the chosen picture at the top of the page. Help students complete the sentence "_____ makes me mad." Then help them write their responses to complete the sentence about what makes them mad, and add the page to their books. Read the sentences together.

▶ Lesson Closing

Have Moe whisper in your ear. **Boys and girls, Moe said that you are so much fun to learn with. Moe has to leave now, but he'll be back tomorrow! Say goodbye to Moe!** Have students say goodbye to Moe verbally or by using their AAC devices.

Lesson 4

Materials

- Moe the frog puppet
- Sight word flashcards: me, is, friend
- 2" × 2" Post-it® notes
- **Level 2 Student Response Book** (pages 90–117)
- Magnetic dry erase board and marker
- **All About Moe** easel book: "Moe Is Happy" story
- "My Book About Me" books completed by students in previous lessons
- "My Book About Me, _____ makes me scared" page in Appendix D
- Pencils, crayons, alphabetic rubber stamps, glue
- Pictures of objects, actions, and events that make the students scared

Optional Materials

- AAC device
- Pointer/light pointer
- Plexiglas® for eye gazing
- Optional pictures or text for AAC device (see Appendix H):
  - Lesson Opening: Good morning, Moe
  - Objective 4: today
  - Objective 14: ______ makes me scared.
  - Lesson Closing: Goodbye, Moe

Tips

- If needed, use the magnetic dry erase board and a marker (or magnetic objects) for reinforcement. Draw a line on the magnet board dividing it into two columns. At the top of the first column, place a picture of the student. At the top of the second column, place a picture of yourself. When a student responds appropriately, congratulate him or her for good work and place a mark on the student side. If a student does not respond appropriately, place a mark on your side. At the end of the lesson, count the marks and find out who had more for that day. Encourage students to participate by being enthusiastic about the marks they received.
- If a student requires an augmentative or alternative communication (AAC) device, preprogram it using the text from the optional materials list.
- All student materials (including AAC overlays and the "My Book About Me" pages) can be printed from Disc 1. Printing from the disc allows you to adapt the materials for students.
- If you are working with a student whose mode of responding is to eye-gaze, the student response options can be printed from Disc 1, laminated, and cut apart. The student choices can be adhered to Plexiglas® with Velcro®. Point to the correct answer after the student gazes to it to provide the watching peers with feedback.

▶ Lesson Opening

Engage the students by welcoming Moe to the class. Say, **Good morning, Moe. Boys and girls, our friend Moe is back for another visit today. Can you say good morning to Moe? Get ready. Good morning, Moe. Again, good morning, Moe. Say it by yourselves.** Have students call Moe or use their AAC devices to say good morning to Moe. **Great job. In our last lesson, we met Moe's friend Molly. Today we are going to read about Moe and Molly again. But first, let's play the Flashcard Game.**

Objective 1

Read sight words using time-delay instruction

Activity

Flashcard Game

Materials

- Moe the frog puppet
- Sight word flashcards: me, friend, is

Tip

A constant time-delay procedure is used to promote near-errorless responding. If a student is making errors in Round 1, which is the 0-second time-delay round, he or she may need additional practice (outside of this lesson) in imitating your model of choosing the correct response. Using pictures, have the student practice pointing where you point until he or she can do so fluently. If the student makes mistakes in Round 2, which is the 5-second time-delay round, shorten the time before you show the correct answer to 2 seconds. He or she will only have time to answer if certain. The student may also need to practice "wait training" to wait for the response. To do "wait training," use several sheets of different colored paper and say, **Point to the paper.** Have the student wait for you to point to show him or her which sheet.

Instructions

Flashcard Game: Part I. Part I of the Flashcard Game will give students practice saying or pointing to words with guidance.

Round 1: In this round, point to the correct answer as you ask the student to point (0-second time delay).

Lay the sight word flashcards in front of the students. Introduce the activity: **Let's play a game. I'll point to a word, then you point to the same word. Watch me.**

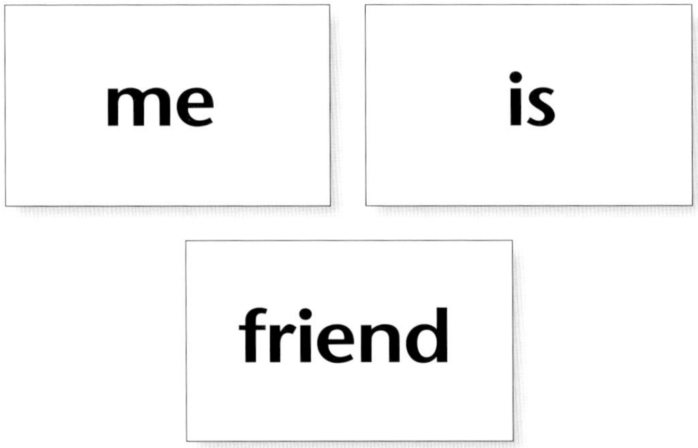

Move the sight word flashcards in front of the first student. Point to the sight word ______ while saying, **This word is ______. (Student name), now you point to ______.**

Be sure you are pointing to the sight word as you say the word. Don't move your finger until the student points to where you are pointing. If you know a student will not imitate you, guide his or her hand for correct responding. For students who eye-gaze, use a light pointer or tap the answer to get them to focus their gaze on the correct answer.

When the student points to ______, say, **Yes, ______.** For students who are verbal, also say, **What word?** and have them say the word.

Wonderful job pointing to the word ______!

Shuffle the sight word flashcards and display them in a new order in front of the next student. In this round, each student takes a

turn pointing to the same sight word before moving on to the next sight word.

(Second student's name), point to ______. Be sure you are pointing to ______ as you say the word. Use the same prompt if required.

After each student's turn, shuffle the sight words around so they are not in the same position. Repeat shuffling sight words and pointing to the words until each student has had a turn with each word. Be sure all students are watching during each student's turn to encourage incidental learning.

Round 2: In Round 2 of the Flashcard Game, students point to or say the sight word independently. Moe is ready to help after giving the student up to 5 seconds to initiate a response (a 5-second time delay).

Have Moe whisper in your ear. **Okeydokey, Moe. We can do that. Moe wants you to find the word. He can help you if you are not sure. (Student's name), find the word ______.**

Allow the student 5 seconds to point to the word. After the student finds the word, have Moe point to the same word with the student. **(Student's name), you point with Moe. Thank you for helping, Moe.**

If the student is verbal, have him or her say the word also. If the student does not point, have Moe prompt the answer and restate the word.

Give each student a turn to practice pointing to the sight word you name. Shuffle the sight words and repeat the process for each student with the remaining words. Be sure all students are watching each other's turn.

Awesome playing the Flashcard Game! Moe is learning to read and so are you! Let's play another game.

Assisting Students

Prompt If the student does not point to the word, use Moe to point to the correct word, saying, **Moe pointed to ______. Now you point to ______.** If the student still does not point, physically guide his or her hand.

Correction If the student points to the wrong word, model the correct response by pointing to the correct word and saying, **This is the word ______. Now you point to ______.** If the student still does not point to the correct word, physically guide his or her hand. Give a turn to another classmate, and praise that student for doing it correctly.

Pile on the Praise

Objective 2

Point to the sight words to complete sentences

Activity

Flashcard Game

Materials

- Moe the frog puppet
- Sight word flashcards: me, friend, is
- **Level 2 Student Response Book** (pages 90–95)

Instructions

Flashcard Game: Part II. Display the Student Response Book. Place Moe's mouth near your ear and appear to be intently listening. **Moe wants you to read your new word in a sentence. Moe, why do you need to read the words in sentences?** Place Moe's mouth near your ear again. **I see . . . that's what the "big frogs" do! The "big frogs" read words in sentences. Then that's what we want to do!**

Model reading sentence A.1 while pointing to each word in the sentence. Place verbal emphasis on the underlined word. **My mom loves me. Listen again. My mom loves me.**

Read sentence B.1, pointing to each word. **My mom loves ______.** Point to the blank space.

Place the sight word flashcards in front of a student, using the correct answer and one distractor. **Show Moe which word goes here** (pointing back to the blank space in the sentence). **What word goes here? ______ or ______?**

Allow the student 5 seconds to respond. If the student responds correctly, affirm by saying, **Yes, me. My mom loves me.**

Shuffle the sight words and repeat the script with sentences A.2 "**My friend is happy**" and B.2, as well as sentences A.3 "**She is at school**" and B.3.

Assisting Students

Prompt If the student does not respond within 5 seconds, read sentence A again, placing verbal emphasis on the sight word. Then read sentence B, pausing at the blank space.

______ is the word that goes here. I can find ______. Point to the correct sight word and say, **(Student's name), point to ______ with me. Yes, ______.**

Correction Do not allow students to practice incorrect responses. For a student who can point and is about to point to an incorrect response, physically guide his or her hand to the correct response while verbally reinforcing the response. For students who use eye-gaze and are visually attending to the incorrect response, remove the incorrect response and visually cue them to the correct response.

Objective 3

Point to text as it is read

Activity

Pointing to Words

Materials

- Moe the frog puppet
- "Moe Is Happy" story
- **Level 2 Student Response Book** (page 96)

Tips

- Use a wait time of 5 seconds for all responses in this activity. However, students may need longer than 5 seconds initially. In this case, responding within 5 seconds should be viewed as a goal to work toward. Note and track response time for any student for whom you feel it is physically difficult to respond within 5 seconds.
- The goal of text pointing in this level is to have students move left-to-right and top-to-bottom.
- Do not slow your speed of reading to accommodate students' speed of movement. Work toward having students keep pace with your speed of reading as they point to the text.

Instructions

Introduce the activity by saying, **Today we are going to read the story "Moe Is Happy."**

While displaying the easel book so all can see, read "Moe Is Happy" with enthusiasm, pointing to the text, moving left-to-right and top-to-bottom while you read.

After reading the story, return to the text-pointing page. Say, **Now Moe needs help reading his story. You can help him. I want you to point to each word in the line that I read. Like this.** While displaying the book so all can see, read lines 4, 5, and 6 of "Moe Is Happy." Point to each word in lines 4, 5, and 6 as you read. Then choose a student to point. Students can point to the text in the story, or you can use the page in the Student Response Book.

(Student's name), your turn! Point to the words for Moe as I read the line. I'm going to show you where to start, and I want you to follow along by pointing to each word as I read it. Show the student where to start pointing by touching the first word.

Repeat for each student, using the lines in the book (or in the Student Response Book).

Let's find out what Moe wants to do next!

Assisting Students

Prompt Modeling for the correct response is already built into the script. A student is given 5 seconds to begin responding. If the student does not initiate a response within 5 seconds, provide a visual cue. A visual cue may be tapping the page in the book and modeling the pointing. If there is still no response within 5 seconds, physically guide the student's hand to point to the words.

Objective 4

Say and/or point to a word to complete a repeated story line

Activity

Hidden Words

Materials

- Moe the frog puppet
- "Moe Is Happy" story (prepare for this activity by adhering a Post-it® note to cover the word *today* highlighted in yellow in story line 5)
- **Level 2 Student Response Book** (page 97)

Tips

- For students who eye-gaze, print the student page from Disc 1 and cut the choices apart. Place the choices a distance apart so that you can discriminate the students' purposeful choices.
- If a student is not able to verbalize, program the AAC device to say the hidden word. Let the student activate the AAC device to say the hidden word and to choose the picture representing the hidden word.

Instructions

Have Moe whisper to you. **Let's play the Hidden Words game! I am going to read a line from the "Moe Is Happy" story, and I will point to a word that is hidden** (covered with the Post-it® note). **Get ready!**

Read line 4 from "Moe Is Happy," emphasizing the word *today*.

Read line 5, pausing to remove the Post-it® note. Point to the word *today* and say, **Today.**

Again cover the word today in line 5. Say, **It's your turn, boys and girls! I am going to read these lines, and this time I want you (or a student's name) to say the hidden word. Get ready!**

Read lines 4 and 5, pausing for a student to indicate the hidden word *today* in line 5. Uncover the word when students say it. Repeat until all students have had a turn.

Now Moe wants you to point to the picture and the word that tells what the hidden word was. First Moe is going to show you how to do it, and then you will have a turn. I will read the lines again, and he will point to a picture that tells what the uncovered word is. He has two choices here.

Point to the pictures in the Student Response Book and tell the students what the two choices are. Read lines 4 and 5, pausing on line 5 for Moe to point to the picture/word representing *today*. Encourage students to say the uncovered word (use an AAC device for nonverbal students). Repeat the sequence for each student.

Assisting Students

Prompt If there is no response within 5 seconds, provide the student with a visual cue. A visual cue might consist of tapping (or using a light pointer to point to) the correct response. Say the word as you give the visual cue. If there is still no response within 5 seconds, physically guide the student's hand to the correct response. Say the word as you give the physical cue.

Objective 5

Respond to literal questions about a story

Activity

Answering Questions

Materials

- Moe the frog puppet
- "Moe Is Happy" story
- **Level 2 Student Response Book** (pages 98–101)

Tips

- Each line is numbered in the story. In this activity, lines 1, 2, 6, and 8 are appropriate places to ask questions. When reading "Moe Is Happy," stop to ask questions at lines 1, 2, 6, and 8. You do not need to ask each student each question; rather, have students take turns answering the questions.
- For students who eye-gaze, print the student page from Disc 1 and cut the choices apart. Place the choices a distance apart so that you can discriminate the students' purposeful choices.

Instructions

Start by having Moe whisper to you. **Moe wants to hear his story again. But this time, I am going to ask you some questions about Moe. You are going to answer the questions by pointing to a picture. The answers are here.** Touch the page in the Student Response Book. **Get ready!**

Read the story "Moe Is Happy," stopping to ask the following questions at the end of the designated lines. After asking the question, point to and name the answer choices in the Student Response Book, and then ask the question again. Encourage students who are verbal to point to the correct response and to say the correct response.

Question 1 from Line 1: **Who is Moe's friend?**
Question 2 from Line 2: **What kind of frog is Molly?**
Question 3 from Line 6: **What did Molly come to do?**
Question 4 from Line 8: **Who sings?**

Assisting Students

Prompt If there is no response within 5 seconds, provide the student with a visual cue. For this skill, you might ask Moe to do the visual prompt (e.g., say, **Moe, can you help [student's name] find the answer?**). A visual cue might consist of having Moe tap the correct response. Say, **Moe has shown you the answer. Now I will read the question again, and you show me the answer.** Read the question a second time. If there is still no response within 5 seconds, physically guide the student's hand to the correct response. Say the word as you give the physical cue.

Correction Do not allow students to practice incorrect responses. For a student who can point and is about to point to an incorrect response, physically guide his or her hand to the correct response while verbally reinforcing the response. For students who use eye-gaze and are visually attending to the incorrect response, remove the incorrect response and visually cue them to the correct response.

Objective 6

Demonstrate understanding of syllable segmentation by clapping out syllables in words

Activity

Chunking Words

Materials

- Moe the frog puppet

Tip

A great deal of thought must be given to how a student who is physically challenged will demonstrate this skill. When providing physical cues, make sure the cue can be faded over time. In order for the cue to be faded, the movement you choose must be one the student can create independently (e.g., don't use clapping as a physical cue if the student is unable to clap independently). One way to determine the best movement for the student to use would be to turn on some music, demonstrate moving to the music, and then watch to see what body part the student is able to move independently.

Instructions

Place Moe's mouth near your ear and appear to be listening intently. **Moe is very shy. He says words in a funny way. He says the sounds in words very slowly. Sometimes it is hard to figure out what he means. Moe wants us to help him. He wants to say the word *happy*. Okeydokey, Moe, you say *happy*.** Listen with concern as Moe says the word *happy*.

Have Moe say, ***Ha...ppy,*** slowly dividing it into two syllables.

Moe said *happy* the slow way. He said *ha...ppy*. I think he is trying to tell us the syllables he hears in *ha...ppy*. Moe, say *happy* again, and we'll clap out the syllables.

Model clapping out the two syllables in the word *happy* as Moe says the word. Make certain that Moe says *happy* slowly, clearly dividing the syllables as he speaks.

Have Moe say, ***Ha...ppy.***

Let's say *happy* again slowly and clap out the syllables for Moe. I'll clap and you help me. *Ha...ppy*. Help me do that again, boys and girls. Repeat the script.

Have Moe whisper in your ear. **Moe wants to try again with more words. Moe, you choose the next word!**

Have Moe say, ***Hel...lo.***

Repeat the above script using ***hello*** and ***today.***

Objective 8

Identify letter-sound correspondences

Activity

Letter Sounds Game

Materials

- Moe the frog puppet
- **Level 2 Student Response Book** (pages 102–104)

Tip

When a letter appears between two virgules (/ /), say the sound the letter makes rather than the letter name (e.g., /s/ means to make the *s* sound). Stretch the sound when multiple letters (e.g., /sss/) appear within the virgules.

Instructions

Letter Sounds Game: Part I. Part I reviews the letter *s* and the sound *s* makes. Introduce the activity: **We are going to play the Letter Sounds Game with a sound you already know. It's a fun game. Get ready!**

Touch below the *s* on the Sound Presentation page in the Student Response Book and say, **This letter says /sss/. The letter *s* says /sss/. Touch /sss/ with me.** Be sure you are pointing below the *s* as you say the sound. Don't move your finger until the student points to where you are pointing. **Your turn. Touch /sss/.** Give each student an opportunity to touch the *s*.

s

102 ELSB Student Response Book • Lesson 4 • Objective 8: Sound Presentation

Letter Sounds Game: Part II. Part II helps students discriminate the *s* sound from two distractors. Introduce the activity: **Now we get to do the next page of the Letter Sounds Game. Get ready!**

Turn to the Letter-Sound Discrimination page in the Student Response Book. **Touch /sss/. Good job touching /sss/. The letter s says /sss/.** Give each student an opportunity to touch the *s*.

Whether students are verbal or nonverbal, encourage them to make the sound for *s*. **This time I will touch the *s* and you say the sound /sss/. Ready?** Give each student an opportunity to say /s/.

For review, repeat the above script for the **short *a*** and ***m*** sounds.

Letter Sounds Game: Part III. Part III helps students identify and discriminate *s* when it is the beginning sound in words.

Turn to the Sam Seal page in the Student Response Book and say, **Our special sound is /sss/. Let's practice. Touch /sss/. Nice touching /sss/. We are going to play a really fun game. First, we will listen to a poem about Sam Seal. Sam Seal swims in**

the sea and then sits on the sand. Let's read the poem about Sam and see if we can hear words that start with /sss/.

Read the following poem one time. While you read, point to the *s* on the Sam Seal page each time you say a word that begins with *s*.

Sam Seal

Sam Seal lives in the sea, and
Sam Seal lives on the land.
Sam swims with flippers to move in the sea
Then sits in the sun and rests on the sand.
Sitting on the sand and swimming in the sea
Sam Seal is somewhat like you . . . and somewhat like me!

I will read the poem again and point to /sss/ when I hear words that begin with /sss/. This time you help me. You touch /sss/ when you hear a word that starts with /sss/.

Read the poem a second time and encourage students to listen and point to the *s* on the Sam Seal page when they hear words that begin with /s/. Stretch the beginning sound to emphasize the *s*. When a student touches the *s* at the appropriate time, give feedback and praise. For example: **Good. The first sound in Sam is /sss/.** Note that students may find it difficult to point to the sound every time they hear it, but even pointing to the sound some of the time helps develop their phonemic awareness.

Assisting Students

Prompt If you know a student will not imitate you, guide his or her hand for correct responding. For students who eye-gaze, use a light pointer or tap the answer to get them to focus their gaze on the correct answer.

Correction Touch below the *s* and say, **This sound is /sss/. Say /sss/ with me. /sss/. Say it by yourself. What sound?**

Objective 9

Point to and/or say the first/last sounds in words

Activity

First/Last Sound Game

Materials

- Moe the frog puppet
- **Level 2 Student Response Book** (page 105)

Tips

- When you say the word the "fast way," touch the colored smiley face to focus students, say "Ready," then slash under the word as you say it.
- Stretch the sound when multiple letters appear in the virgules (e.g., /sss/). Note that some sounds cannot be stretched (e.g., /t/).

Instructions

Place Moe's mouth near your ear and appear to be listening. **Moe wants us to get really good at knowing the first sounds in words. Moe has a fun game to play with colored smiling faces to help us hear the first sounds in words. Okeydokey, Moe! We are ready to play the First/Last Sound Game.**

Touch the green smiley face on the student page. **Get ready to read the word that comes after the green smiley face. I'll touch and say the first sound /sss/. I will touch and say the next sound /aaa/. Then I will touch and say the last sound /t/. Say the sounds in this word with me /sss/ /aaa/ /t/.**

I can say this word the fast way. Ready (put your finger on the smiley face, then say *sat* without segmenting it into sounds), ***sat*. Say this word the fast way with me, *sat*. Yes, *sat*. We said *sat* the fast way.**

Touch the first sound in *sat*. Say, **The first sound in *sat* is /sss/. Touch the first sound in *sat*.** Have a student touch or point to *s*.

Say the first sound in *sat*. Place emphasis on the beginning sound when you say the word *sat*. **Yes, /sss/ is the first sound in the word *sat*.**

Repeat the script above for: **at, sam, man,** changing the script to match the color of the smiley face and the beginning sound you are focusing on.

Assisting Students

Prompt If you know a student will not imitate you, guide his or her hand for correct responding. For students who eye-gaze, use a light pointer or tap the answer to get them to focus their gaze on the correct answer.

Correction Touch below each sound and say, **This sound is /___/. Say /___/ with me. /___/. Say it by yourself. What sound?.**

Objective 10

Identify pictures that begin/end with given sounds

Activity

Finding Pictures with Special Sounds

Materials

- Moe the frog puppet
- **Level 2 Student Response Book** (pages 106–109)

Instructions

Place Moe's mouth near your ear and appear to be listening. **Moe is ready to play his game Finding Pictures with Special Sounds. The special sounds today are /sss/, /mmm/, and /aaa/.**

Display the Student Response Book. Point to each picture as you name it (tape, mop, sick, bear), placing emphasis on the first sound in each word.

Say the picture words with me. The first sound in *tape* is /t/. The first sound in *mop* is /m/. The first sound in *sick* is /s/. The first sound in *bear* is /b/.

Point to the picture that has /mmm/ as its first sound. Show me the picture that starts with /mmm/.

Have a student point to the mop. **Yes, the first sound in the word *mop* is /mmm/.**

Repeat the above script for each student page. Change the script to match the target sound. The target response (focusing on either /m/, /a/, or /s/) has an asterisk in the list below.

jam, boy, *man, fish,
ball, horse, sink, *ant
***sock, nail, cat, bike**

Give all students 5 seconds to respond after you say, **Show me the picture that starts with ___.**

Assisting Students

Prompt and Correction

If there is no response within 5 seconds, point to the correct response and say, **The first sound in ___ is /___/. Touch the picture of ______.** If the student does not respond within 5 seconds, physically guide the student's hand to the correct response and say, ___ **starts with /___/.**

Objective 13

Point to pictures/words representing new vocabulary

Activity

The New Word Game

Materials

- Moe the frog puppet
- **Level 2 Student Response Book** (pages 110–117)

Instructions

Introduce the activity: **Sometimes Moe is happy, sometimes Moe is sad, and sometimes Moe gets really mad! Sometimes I get mad, too. If people are mean to my students, I get mad!** Have Moe whisper in your ear. **Moe wants me to tell you a secret. Sometimes at night when it is really dark, Moe says that he feels "scared!" I'm sorry, Moe. Sometimes I am scared, too. The first time I went swimming, I was scared. One time a big dog chased me and I was very scared! Have you ever been scared? Let's look at some pictures of people who are scared.**

Open the Student Response Book and point to each picture for scared. Say, **This person is scared. And this person is scared. This person is scared, too.**

Give each student a turn to point to a picture of someone who is scared. Say, **(Student's name), point to scared.** If the student does not point, point to a picture and repeat the direction. If needed, physically guide the student's hand, saying, **This is scared.**

Give each student a turn, pointing to each picture of someone who is scared with each turn.

Turn to the next three student pages, which have *scared* and three distractors, and say, **OK, I'm trying to trick you! Point to the picture of scared.**

Give each student a turn. Use prompts as necessary.

Turn to the next four student pages and repeat the above script with: **mad.**

End the activity by saying, **Great job! Now let's use these words to write another page in your books about you.**

Assisting Students

Prompt If the student does not point to the picture, physically guide his or her hand, saying, **This is scared (mad).**

Correction If the student points to the wrong picture, model pointing to the correct picture, saying, **This is scared (mad). Now you point to scared (mad).** If the student still does not point to the correct picture, physically guide his or her hand. Give a turn to another classmate, and praise that student for doing it correctly.

Objective 14

Use new vocabulary words and personal information to create a story

Activity

Fun with Writing

Materials

- "My Book About Me" books completed by students in previous lessons
- "My Book About Me, _____ makes me scared" page in Appendix D
- Pencils, crayons, rubber alphabet stamps, glue
- Pictures of objects, actions, or events that make the students scared

Tips

- If a student is not able to write, have the student ask someone to write for him or her. If the student is not verbal, program an AAC device to state, "_____ makes me scared." You can also create each student's response to what makes him or her scared using a word processor and print in a size that will fit on the page. Students can also use the rubber alphabet stamps to stamp their responses.
- If the student is not able to read the sentences in their books, program an AAC device to read the sentences or to read the new sentence.
- If a student is not able to verbalize for the lesson closing, use an AAC device to say, "Goodbye, Moe."

Instructions

In this activity, students complete another page of their "My Book About Me" books by stamping their response to what makes them scared at the beginning of the first sentence, by writing their responses with your assistance, or by gluing their responses (which have been prepared) on the line.

Introduce the activity: **Remember that you started making a book that was all about you! Today you are going to add another page to your book. But first, you have to find your books.**

Lay out the "My Book About Me" books, asking students to identify their own. Review their book covers by reading the titles and pointing to the words as you read. Have each student point to their photos on the front of their books. Have students reread the pages of their books. Then present the pictures of objects, actions, and events that make them scared.

Say, **Pick a picture of something that makes you scared.**

Distribute the new "My Book About Me" page. Help them glue the chosen picture at the top of the page. Help students complete the sentence "______ makes me scared." Then help them write their responses to complete the sentence about what makes them scared, and add the page to their books. Read the sentences together.

Lesson Closing

Have Moe whisper in your ear. **Boys and girls, Moe said you are awesome learners. Moe has to leave now, but he'll be back tomorrow! Say goodbye to Moe!** Have students say goodbye to Moe verbally or by using their AAC devices.

Lesson 5

Materials

- Moe the frog puppet
- Sight word flashcards: me, is, friend
- 2" × 2" Post-it® notes
- **Level 2 Student Response Book** (pages 118–145)
- Magnetic dry erase board and marker
- **All About Moe** easel book: "Moe Is Not Happy" and "Moe Is Happy" stories
- "My Book About Me" books completed by students in previous lessons
- "My Book About Me, _____ makes me excited" page in Appendix D
- Pencils, crayons, alphabetic rubber stamps, glue
- Pictures of objects, actions, and events that make the students excited

Optional Materials

- AAC device
- Pointer/light pointer
- Plexiglas® for eye gazing
- Optional pictures or text for AAC device (see Appendix H):
  - Lesson Opening: Hello, Moe
  - Objective 4: sings
  - Objective 14: ______ makes me excited.
  - Lesson Closing: Goodbye, Moe

Tips

- If needed, use the magnetic dry erase board and a marker (or magnetic objects) for reinforcement. Draw a line on the magnet board dividing it into two columns. At the top of the first column, place a picture of the student. At the top of the second column, place a picture of yourself. When a student responds appropriately, congratulate him or her for good work and place a mark on the student side. If a student does not respond appropriately, place a mark on your side. At the end of the lesson, count the marks and find out who had more for that day. Encourage students to participate by being enthusiastic about the marks they received.

- If a student requires an augmentative or alternative communication (AAC) device, preprogram it using the text from the optional materials list.

- All student materials (including AAC overlays and the "My Book About Me" pages) can be printed from Disc 1. Printing from the disc allows you to adapt the materials for students.

- If you are working with a student whose mode of responding is to eye-gaze, the student response options can be printed from Disc 1, laminated, and cut apart. The student choices can be adhered to Plexiglas® with Velcro®. Point to the correct answer after the student gazes to it to provide the watching peers with feedback.

▶ Lesson Opening

Engage students by welcoming Moe to the class. Say, **Hello, Moe! Boys and girls, our friend Moe is back for another visit today. Can you say hello to Moe? Get ready . . . Hello, Moe! Again, Hello, Moe! Say it by yourselves.** Have students call Moe or use their AAC devices to say hello to Moe. **Great job! Today, we are going to read two stories about Moe. We will read the story "Moe Is Not Happy" and then we will read the story "Moe Is Happy." First we'll play the Flashcard Game.**

Objective 1

Read sight words using time-delay instruction

Activity

Flashcard Game

Materials

- Moe the frog puppet
- Sight word flashcards: me, is, friend

Tip

A constant time-delay procedure is used to promote near-errorless responding. If a student is making errors in Round 1, which is the 0-second time-delay round, he or she may need additional practice (outside of this lesson) in imitating your model of choosing the correct response. Using pictures, have the student practice pointing where you point until he or she can do so fluently. If the student makes mistakes in Round 2, which is the 5-second time-delay round, shorten the time before you show the correct answer to 2 seconds. He or she will only have time to answer if certain. The student may also need to practice "wait training" to wait for the response. To do "wait training," use several sheets of different colored paper and say, **Point to the paper.** Have the student wait for you to point to show him or her which sheet.

Instructions

Flashcard Game: Part I. Part I of the Flashcard Game will give students practice saying or pointing to words with guidance.

Round 1: In this round, point to the correct answer as you ask the student to point (0-second time delay).

Lay the sight word flashcards in front of the students. Introduce the activity: **Let's play a game. I'll point to a word, then you point to the same word. Watch me.**

me	**is**
friend	

Move the sight word flashcards in front of the first student. Point to the sight word ______ while saying, **This word is ______. (Student name), now you point to ______.**

Be sure you are pointing to the sight word as you say the word. Don't move your finger until the student points to where you are pointing. If you know a student will not imitate you, guide his or her hand for correct responding. For students who eye-gaze, use a light pointer or tap the answer to get them to focus their gaze on the correct answer.

When the student points to ______, say, **Yes, ______.** For students who are verbal, also say, **What word?** and have them say the word.

Wonderful job pointing to the word ______!

Shuffle the sight word flashcards and display them in a new order in front of the next student. In this round, each student takes a

turn pointing to the same sight word before moving on to the next sight word.

(Second student's name), point to ______. Be sure you are pointing to ______ as you say the word. Use the same prompt if required.

After each student's turn, shuffle the sight words around so they are not in the same position. Repeat shuffling sight words and pointing to the words until each student has had a turn with each word. Be sure all students are watching during each student's turn to encourage incidental learning.

Round 2: In Round 2 of the Flashcard Game, students point to or say the sight word independently. Moe is ready to help after giving the student up to 5 seconds to initiate a response (a 5-second time delay).

Have Moe whisper in your ear. **Okeydokey, Moe. We can do that. Moe wants you to find the word. He can help you if you are not sure. (Student's name), find the word ______.**

Allow the student 5 seconds to point to the word. After the student finds the word, have Moe point to the same word with the student. **(Student's name), you point with Moe. Thank you for helping, Moe.**

If the student is verbal, have him or her say the word also. If the student does not point, have Moe prompt the answer and restate the word.

Give each student a turn to practice pointing to the sight word you name. Shuffle the sight words and repeat the process for each student with the remaining words. Be sure all students are watching each other's turn.

Awesome playing the Flashcard Game! Moe is learning to read and so are you! Let's play the next game.

Assisting Students

Prompt If the student does not point to the word, use Moe to point to the correct word, saying, **Moe pointed to ______. Now you point to ______.** If the student still does not point, physically guide his or her hand.

Correction If the student points to the wrong word, model the correct response by pointing to the correct word and saying, **This is the word ______. Now you point to ______.** If the student still does not point to the correct word, physically guide his or her hand. Give a turn to another classmate, and praise that student for doing it correctly.

Pile on the Praise

Objective 2

Point to the sight words to complete sentences

Activity

Flashcard Game

Materials

- Moe the frog puppet
- Sight word flashcards: me, is, friend
- **Level 2 Student Response Book** (pages 118–123)

Instructions

Flashcard Game: Part II. Display the Student Response Book. Place Moe's mouth near your ear and appear to be intently listening. **Moe wants you to read your new word in a sentence. Moe, why do you need to read the words in sentences?** Place Moe's mouth near your ear again. **I see . . . that's what the "big frogs" do! The "big frogs" read words in sentences. Then that's what we want to do!**

Model reading sentence A.1 while pointing to each word in the sentence. Place verbal emphasis on the underlined word. **Please show me. Listen again. Please show me.**

Read sentence B.1, pointing to each word. **Please show ______.** Point to the blank space.

Place the sight word flashcards in front of a student, using the correct answer and one distractor. **Show Moe which word goes here** (pointing back to the blank space in the sentence). **What word goes here? ______ or ______?**

Allow the student 5 seconds to respond. If the student responds correctly, affirm by saying, **Yes, me. Please show me.**

Shuffle the sight words and repeat the script with sentences A.2 "**Ms. Grey is my teacher**" and B.2, as well as sentences A.3 "**Monique is her friend**" and B.3

Assisting Students

Prompt If the student does not respond within 5 seconds, read sentence A again, placing verbal emphasis on the sight word. Then read sentence B, pausing at the blank space.

______ is the word that goes here. I can find ______. Point to the correct sight word and say, **(Student's name), point to ______ with me. Yes, ______.**

Correction Do not allow students to practice incorrect responses. For a student who can point and is about to point to an incorrect response, physically guide his or her hand to the correct response while verbally reinforcing the response. For students who use eye-gaze and are visually attending to the incorrect response, remove the incorrect response and visually cue them to the correct response.

Objective 3

Point to text as it is read

Activity

Pointing to Words

Materials

- Moe the frog puppet
- "Moe Is Not Happy" and "Moe Is Happy" stories
- **Level 2 Student Response Book** (page 124)

Tips

- Use a wait time of 5 seconds for all responses in this activity. However, students may need longer than 5 seconds initially. In this case, responding within 5 seconds should be viewed as a goal to work toward. Note and track response time for any student for whom you feel it is physically difficult to respond within 5 seconds.
- The goal of text pointing in this level is to have students move left-to-right and top-to-bottom.
- Do not slow your speed of reading to accommodate students' speed of movement. Work toward having students keep pace with your speed of reading as they point to the text.

Instructions

Introduce the activity by saying, **Today we are going to read the stories "Moe Is Not Happy" and "Moe Is Happy."**

While displaying the easel book so all can see, read "Moe Is Not Happy" with enthusiasm, pointing to the text, moving left-to-right and top-to-bottom while you read. Then read "Moe Is Happy" with enthusiasm, also pointing to the text as you read.

After reading the story, return to the text-pointing page. Say, **Now Moe needs help reading "Moe Is Happy." You can help him. I want you to point to each word in the lines that I read, like this.** While displaying "Moe Is Happy" so all can see, read lines 7, 8, 9, and 10. Point to each word in lines 7, 8, 9, and 10 as you read. Then choose a student to point. Students can point to the text in the story, or you can use the page in the Student Response Book.

(Student's name), your turn! Point to the words for Moe as I read the line. I'm going to show you where to start, and I want you to follow along by pointing to each word as I read it. Show the student where to start pointing by touching the first word.

Repeat for each student, using the lines in the book (or in the Student Response Book).

Let's find out what Moe wants to do next!

Assisting Students

Prompt Modeling for the correct response is already built into the script. A student is given 5 seconds to begin responding. If the student does not initiate a response within 5 seconds, provide a visual cue. A visual cue may be tapping the page in the book and modeling the pointing. If there is still no response within 5 seconds, physically guide the student's hand to point to the words.

Objective 4

Say and/or point to a word to complete a repeated story line

Activity

Hidden Words

Materials

- Moe the frog puppet
- "Moe Is Happy" story (prepare for this activity by adhering a Post-it® note to cover the word *sings* highlighted in yellow in story line 8)
- **Level 2 Student Response Book** (page 125)

Tips

- For students who eye-gaze, print the student page from Disc 1 and cut the choices apart. Place the choices a distance apart so that you can discriminate the student's purposeful choices.
- If a student is not able to verbalize, program the AAC device to say the hidden word. Let the student activate the AAC device to say the hidden word and to choose the picture representing the hidden word.

Instructions

Have Moe whisper to you. **Let's play the Hidden Words game! I am going to read a line from the "Moe Is Happy" story, and I will point to a word that is hidden** (covered with the Post-it® note). **Get ready!**

Read line 7 from "Moe Is Happy," emphasizing the word *sings.*

Read line 8, pausing to remove the Post-it® note. Point to the word *sings* and say, **Sings.**

Again cover the word *sings* in line 8. Say, **It's your turn, boys and girls! I am going to read these lines, and this time I want you (or a student's name) to say the hidden word. Get ready!**

Read lines 7 and 8, pausing for a student to indicate the hidden word *sings* in line 8. Uncover the word when students say it. Repeat until all students have had a turn.

Now Moe wants you to point to the picture and the word that tells what the hidden word was. First Moe is going to show you how to do it and then you will have a turn. I will read the lines again, and he will point to a picture that tells what the uncovered word is. He has two choices here.

Point to the pictures in the Student Response Book and tell the students what the two choices are. Read lines 7 and 8, pausing on line 8 for Moe to point to the picture/word representing *sings.* Encourage students to say the uncovered word (use an AAC device for nonverbal students). Repeat the sequence for each student.

Assisting Students

Prompt If there is no response within 5 seconds, provide the student with a visual cue. A visual cue might consist of tapping (or using a light pointer to point to) the correct response. Say the word as you give the visual cue. If there is still no response within 5 seconds, physically guide the student's hand to the correct response. Say the word as you give the physical cue.

Objective 5

Respond to literal questions about a story

Activity

Answering Questions

Materials

- Moe the frog puppet
- "Moe Is Not Happy" and "Moe Is Happy" stories
- **Level 2 Student Response Book** (pages 126–129)

Tips

- Each line is numbered in the story. In this activity, lines 9 and 10 in "Moe Is Not Happy" and lines 6 and 10 in "Moe Is Happy" are appropriate places to ask questions. When reading, stop to ask questions at lines 9 and 10 in "Moe Is Not Happy" and lines 6 and 10 in "Moe Is Happy." You do not need to ask each student each question; rather, have students take turns answering the questions.

- For students who eye-gaze, print the student page from Disc 1 and cut the choices apart. Place the choices a distance apart so that you can discriminate the students' purposeful choices.

Instructions

Start by having Moe whisper to you. **Moe wants to hear both of his stories again. But this time, I am going to ask you some questions about Moe. You are going to answer the questions by pointing to a picture. The answers are here.** Touch the page in the Student Response Book. **Get ready!**

Read the stories, stopping to ask the following questions at the end of the designated lines. After asking the question, point to and name the answer choices in the Student Response Book, and then ask the question again. Encourage students who are verbal to point to the correct response and to say the correct response.

Question 1 from "Moe Is Not Happy," Line 9: **What does Moe want?**
Question 2 from "Moe Is Not Happy," Line 10: **What does Moe do?**
Question 3 from "Moe Is Happy," Line 6: **Who came to play with Moe?**
Question 4 from "Moe Is Happy," Line 10: **Who is happy?**

Assisting Students

Prompt If there is no response within 5 seconds, provide the student with a visual cue. For this skill, you might ask Moe to do the visual prompt (e.g., say, **Moe, can you help [student's name] find the answer?**). A visual cue might consist of having Moe tap the correct response. Say, **Moe has shown you the answer. Now I will read the question again, and you show me the answer.** Read the question a second time. If there is still no response within 5 seconds, physically guide the student's hand to the correct response. Say the word as you give the physical cue.

Correction Do not allow students to practice incorrect responses. For a student who can point and is about to point to an incorrect response, physically guide his or her hand to the correct response while verbally reinforcing the response. For students who use eye-gaze and are visually attending to the incorrect response, remove the incorrect response and visually cue them to the correct response.

Objective 6

Demonstrate understanding of syllable segmentation by clapping out syllables in words

Activity

Chunking Words

Materials

- Moe the frog puppet

Tip

A great deal of thought must be given to how a student who is physically challenged will demonstrate this skill. When providing physical cues, make sure the cue can be faded over time. In order for the cue to be faded, the movement you choose must be one the student can create independently (e.g., Don't use clapping as a physical cue if the student is unable to clap independently). One way to determine the best movement for the student to use would be to turn on some music, demonstrate moving to the music, and then watch to see what body part the student is able to move independently.

Instructions

Place Moe's mouth near your ear and appear to be listening intently. **Moe is very shy. He says words in a funny way. He says the sounds in words very slowly. Sometimes it is hard to figure out what he means. Moe wants us to help him. He wants to say Molly's name. Okeydokey, Moe, you say her name, *Molly*.** Listen with concern as Moe says the name *Molly*.

Have Moe say, ***Mo...lly,*** slowly dividing it into two syllables.

Moe said *Molly* the slow way. He said *Mo...lly*. I think he is trying to tell us the syllables he hears in *Mo...lly*. Moe, say *Molly* again, and we'll clap out the syllables.

Model clapping out the two syllables in the word *Molly* as Moe says the word. Make certain that Moe says *Molly* slowly, clearly dividing the syllables as he speaks.

Have Moe say, ***Mo...lly.***

Let's say *Molly* again slowly and clap out the syllables for Moe. I'll clap and you help me. *Mo...lly*. Help me do that again, boys and girls. Repeat the script.

Have Moe whisper in your ear. **Moe wants to try again with more words. Moe, you choose the next word!**

Have Moe say, ***Jump...ing.***

Repeat the above script using ***jumping,*** **your name**, and **students' names** that are two to three syllables in length.

Objective 8

Identify letter-sound correspondences

Activity

Letter Sounds Game

Materials

- Moe the frog puppet
- **Level 2 Student Response Book** (pages 130–132)

Tip

When a letter appears between two virgules (/ /), say the sound the letter makes rather than the letter name (e.g., /m/ means to make the *m* sound). Stretch the sound when multiple letters (e.g., /mmm/) appear within the virgules.

Instructions

Letter Sounds Game: Part I. Part I reviews the letter m and the sound m makes. Introduce the activity: **We are going to play the Letter Sounds Game with a sound you already know. It's a fun game. Get ready!**

Touch below the *m* on the Sound Presentation page in the Student Response Book and say, **This letter says /mmm/. The letter *m* says /mmm/. Touch /mmm/ with me.** Be sure you are pointing below the *m* as you say the sound. Don't move your finger until the student points to where you are pointing. **Your turn. Touch /mmm/.** Give each student an opportunity to touch the *m*.

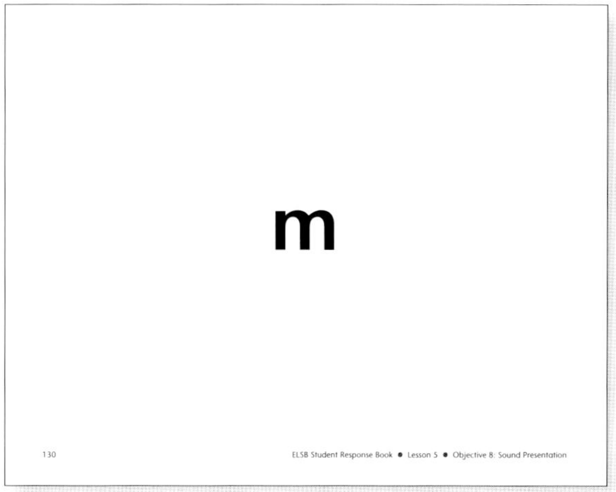

Letter Sounds Game: Part II. Part II helps students discriminate the *m* sound from two distractors. Introduce the activity: **Now we get to do the next page of the Letter Sounds Game. Get ready!**

Turn to the Letter-Sound Discrimination page in the Student Response Book. **Touch /mmm/. Good job touching /mmm/. The letter *m* says /mmm/.** Give each student an opportunity to touch the *m*.

Whether students are verbal or nonverbal, encourage them to make the sound for *m*. **This time I will touch the *m* and you say the sound /mmm/. Ready?** Give each student an opportunity to say /m/.

For review, repeat the above script for the **short *a*** and ***s*** sounds.

Letter Sounds Game: Part III. Part III helps students identify and discriminate *s* when it is the beginning sound in words.

Turn to the Millie Monkey page in the Student Response Book and say, **Our special sound is /mmm/. Let's practice. Touch /mmm/. Nice touching /mmm/. We are going to play a really fun game. First, we will listen to the silly poem about Millie Monkey. Millie**

lives at the Miami zoo. Let's read the poem about Millie and see if we can hear words that start with /mmm/.

Read the following poem one time. While you read, point to the *m* on the Millie Monkey page each time you say a word that begins with *m*.

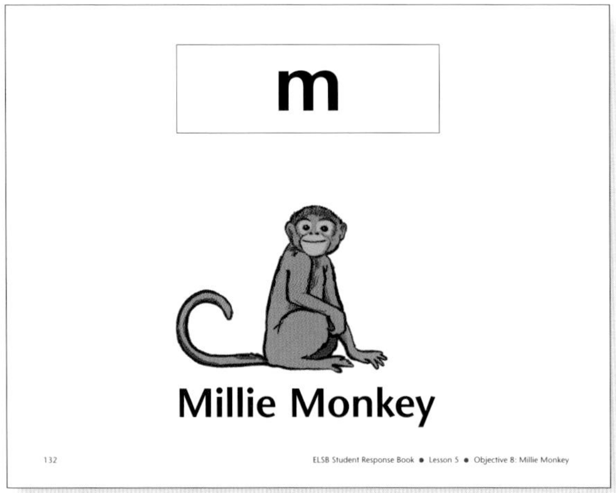

Millie Monkey

Millie **M**onkey lives at the **M**iami zoo,
With her **m**ama and her papa and some cousins, too!
Millie and **M**ama play on the **m**onkey swing.
Millie pushes **M**ama high on the swing.
Mama swings up and a bell starts to ring.
Mama pushes **M**illie high on the swing.
Millie swings high and **M**illie swings low,
Down to the ground . . . then up she goes!
Up . . . goes **M**illie.
The bell starts to ring.
Then down jumps **M**illie from the **m**onkey swing!

I will read the poem again and point to /mmm/ when I hear words that begin with /mmm/. This time you help me. You touch /mmm/ when you hear a word that starts with /mmm/.

Read the poem a second time and encourage students to listen and point to the *m* on the Millie Monkey page when they hear words that begin with /m/. Stretch the beginning sound to emphasize the *m*. When a student touches the *m* at the appropriate time, give feedback and praise. For example: **Good. The first sound in Millie is /mmm/.** Note that students may find it difficult to point to the sound every time they hear it, but even pointing to the sound some of the time helps develop their phonemic awareness.

Assisting Students

Prompt If you know a student will not imitate you, guide his or her hand for correct responding. For students who eye-gaze, use a light pointer or tap the answer to get them to focus their gaze on the correct answer.

Correction Touch below the *m* and say, **This sound is /mmm/. Say /mmm/ with me. /mmm/. Say it by yourself. What sound?**

Objective 9

Point to and/or say the first/last sounds in words

Activity

First/Last Sound Game

Materials

- Moe the frog puppet
- **Level 2 Student Response Book** (page 133)

Tips

- When you say the word the "fast way," touch the colored smiley face to focus students, say "Ready," then slash under the word as you say it.
- Stretch the sound when multiple letters appear in the virgules (e.g., /aaa/). Note that some sounds cannot be stretched (e.g., /t/).

Instructions

Place Moe's mouth near your ear and appear to be listening. **Moe wants us to get really good at knowing the first sounds in words. Moe has a fun game to play with colored smiling faces to help us hear the first sounds in words. OK, Moe! We are ready to play the First/Last Sound Game.**

Touch the green smiley face on the student page. **Get ready to read the word that comes after the green smiley face. I'll touch and say the first sound /aaa/. Then I will touch and say the last sound /t/. Say the sounds in this word with me: /aaa/ /t/.**

I can say this word the fast way. Ready (put your finger on the smiley face, then say *at* without segmenting it into sounds), ***at.***

Say this word the fast way with me, *at*. Yes, *at*. We said *at* the fast way.

Touch the first sound in *at*. Say, **The first sound in *at* is /aaa/. Touch the first sound in *at*.** Have a student touch or point to *a*.

Say the first sound in *at*. Place emphasis on the beginning sound when you say the word *at*. **Yes, /aaa/ is the first sound in the word *at*.**

Repeat the script above for: **man, sam, am,** changing the script to match the color of the smiley face and the beginning sound you are focusing on.

Assisting Students

Prompt If you know a student will not imitate you, guide his or her hand for correct responding. For students who eye-gaze, use a light pointer or tap the answer to get them to focus their gaze on the correct answer.

Correction Touch below each sound and say, **This sound is /___/. Say /___/ with me. /___/. Say it by yourself. What sound?**

Objective 10

Identify pictures that begin/end with given sounds

Activity

Finding Pictures with Special Sounds

Materials

- Moe the frog puppet
- **Level 2 Student Response Book** (pages 134–137)

Instructions

Place Moe's mouth near your ear and appear to be listening. **Moe is ready to play his game Finding Pictures with Special Sounds. The special sounds today are /mmm/, /aaa/, and /sss/.**

Display the Student Response Book. Point to each picture as you name it (fan, milk, rose, bee), placing emphasis on the first sound in each word.

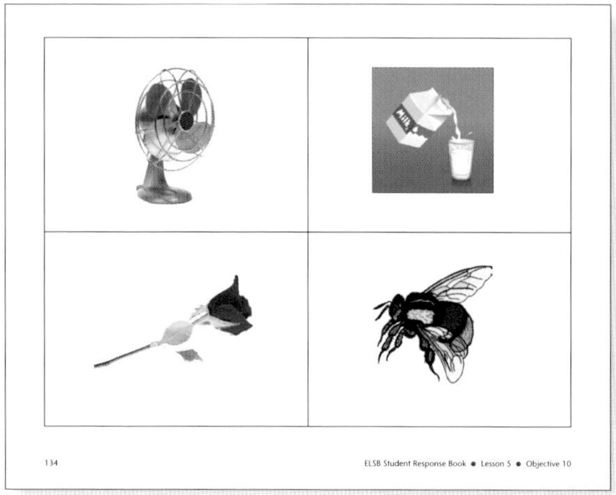

Say the picture words with me. The first sound in *fan* is /fff/. The first sound in *milk* is /mmm/. /The first sound in *rose* is /rrr/. The first sound in *bee* is /b/.

Point to the picture that has /mmm/ as its first sound. Show me the picture that starts with /mmm/.

Have a student point to the milk. **Yes, the first sound in the word *milk* is /mmm/.**

Repeat the above script for each student page. Change the script to match the target sound. The target response (focusing on either /m/, /a/, or /s/) has an asterisk in the list below.

***man, tent, foot, jam**
sun, boy, *ant, horse
***sock, pie, bat, lion**

Give all students 5 seconds to respond after you say, **Show me the picture that starts with ______.**

Assisting Students

Prompt and Correction

If there is no response within 5 seconds, point to the correct response and say, **The first sound in ______ is /___/. Touch the picture of ______.** If the student does not respond within 5 seconds, physically guide the student's hand to the correct response and say, ______ **starts with /___/.**

Objective 13

Point to pictures/words representing new vocabulary

Activity

The New Word Game

Materials

- Moe the frog puppet
- **Level 2 Student Response Book** (pages 138–145)

Instructions

Introduce the activity: **Sometimes Moe is happy and sometimes Moe is sad. Yesterday Moe told me that sometimes at night when he is all alone, he gets scared. Moe, how are you feeling today?**

Have Moe say, **Excited.**

Moe is excited because he is learning to read. Awesome! We are excited about that, too, and do you know what? We are learning to read, too. That is exciting. Let's learn a new word.

Open the Student Response Book and point to each picture for excited. Say, **This person is excited. And this person is excited. This person is excited, too.**

Give each student a turn to point to a picture of someone who is excited. Say, **(Student's name), point to excited.** If the student does not point, point to a picture and repeat the direction. If needed, physically guide the student's hand, saying, **This is excited.**

Give each student a turn, pointing to a picture of someone who is excited with each turn.

Turn to the next three student pages, which have *excited* and three distractors, and say, **OK, I'm trying to trick you! Point to the picture of excited.**

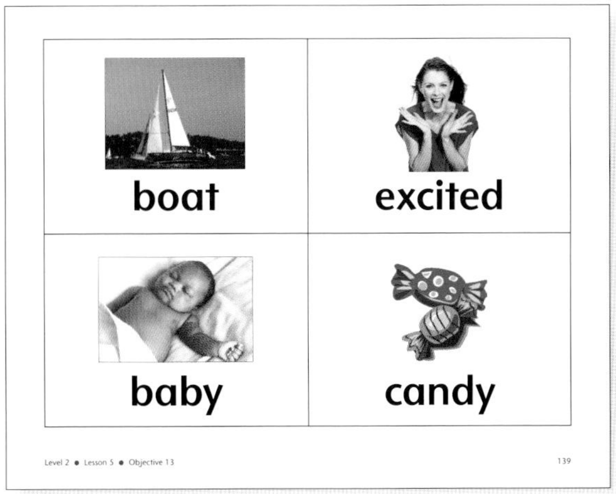

Give each student a turn. Use prompts as necessary.

Turn to the next four student pages and repeat the above script with: **scared.**

End the activity by saying, **Great job! Now let's use these words to write another page in your books about you.**

Assisting Students

Prompt If the student does not point to the picture, physically guide his or her hand, saying, **This is excited (scared).**

Correction If the student points to the wrong picture, model pointing to the correct picture, saying, **This is excited (scared). Now you point to excited (scared).** If the student still does not point to the correct picture, physically guide his or her hand. Give a turn to another classmate, and praise that student for doing it correctly.

Objective 14

Use new vocabulary words and personal information to create a story

Activity

Fun with Writing

Materials

- "My Book About Me" books completed by students in previous lessons
- "My Book About Me, _____ makes me excited" page in Appendix D
- Pencils, crayons, rubber alphabet stamps, glue
- Pictures of objects, actions, or events that make the students excited

Tips

- If a student is not able to write, have the student ask someone to write for him or her. If the student is not verbal, program an AAC device to state, "______ makes me excited." You can also create each student's response to what makes him or her excited using a word processor and print in a size that will fit on the page. Students can also use the rubber alphabet stamps to stamp their responses.
- If the student is not able to read the sentences in their books, program an AAC device to read the sentences or to read the new sentence.
- If a student is not able to verbalize for the lesson closing, use an AAC device to say, "Goodbye, Moe."

Instructions

In this activity, students complete another page of their "My Book About Me" books by stamping their response to what makes them excited at the beginning of the first sentence, by writing their responses with your assistance, or by gluing their responses (which have been prepared) on the line.

Introduce the activity: **Remember that you started making a book that was all about you! Today you are going to add another page to your book. But first, you have to find your books.**

Lay out the "My Book About Me" books, asking students to identify their own. Review their book covers by reading the titles and pointing to the words as you read. Have each student point to their photos on the front of their books. Have students reread the pages of their books. Then present the pictures of objects, actions, and events that make them excited.

Say, **Pick a picture of something that makes you excited.**

Distribute the new "My Book About Me" page. Help them glue the chosen picture at the top of the page. Help students complete the sentence "______ makes me excited." Then help them write their responses to complete the sentence about what makes them excited, and add the page to their books. Read the sentences together.

▶ Lesson Closing

Have Moe whisper in your ear. **Boys and girls, Moe said he is excited that you are learning to read! Moe has to leave now, but he'll be back tomorrow! Say goodbye to Moe!** Have students say goodbye to Moe verbally or by using their AAC devices.

Level 3

Level 3 Scope and Sequence

Objective	Activity	Lesson 1	Lesson 2	Lesson 3	Lesson 4	Lesson 5
1. Read sight words using time-delay instruction	Flashcard Game	want, he, is, boy	want, he, is, boy	want, he, is, boy	want, he, is, boy	want, he, is, boy
2. Point to the sight words to complete sentences	Flashcard Game	I really want a dog. He is going to the pet store. Moe is excited. The boy wants a snake.	I want a bird. Moe doesn't know which pet he wants. The rabbit is soft. The boy found a turtle.	How much do you want? First he saw a dog. Moe is a frog. Jason is a boy.	I want a cat. He can swim. Where is my book? I like that boy.	I don't want to play. He is going to school. She is going to the park. That boy can sing.
3. Point to text as it is read	Pointing to Words	Read "Moe Wants a Pet." Students point to text in lines 1–3.	Read "Moe Wants a Pet." Students point to text in lines 6–8.	Read "Moe Gets a Pet." Students point to text in lines 1–3.	Read "Moe Gets a Pet." Students point to text in lines 6–9.	Read "Moe Wants a Pet." Read "Moe Gets a Pet." Students point to text in lines 8–11 in "Moe Gets a Pet."
4. Say and/or point to a word to complete a repeated story line (Note that Level 3 phases out highlighting of words)	Hidden Words	Repeated word: pet	Repeated word: dog	Repeated word: dog	Repeated word: cat	Repeated word: one

Objective	Activity	Lesson 1	Lesson 2	Lesson 3	Lesson 4	Lesson 5
5. Respond to literal questions about a story	Answering Questions	"Moe Wants a Pet" After viewing the cover: What do you think this story is going to be about? Line 1: Who is excited? Line 2: What kind of store is Moe going to? Line 6: What pet could Moe get?	"Moe Wants a Pet" Line 1: How does Moe feel? Line 2: How many pets can Moe get? Line 9: Does Moe want a cat, a dog, or a goat? After reading the entire story: What was the story about?	"Moe Gets a Pet" After viewing the cover: What do you think this story is going to be about? Line 1: Where did Moe go? Line 3: What did Moe see first? Line 10: What pet did Moe get?	"Moe Gets a Pet" Line 3: What was the dog sitting on? Line 5: Who could get only one pet? Line 8: How many pets could Moe get? After reading the entire story: What was the story about?	"Moe Wants a Pet" Line 2: Who is going to the pet store? Line 7: What pet does Moe want? "Moe Gets a Pet" Line 9: How many pets can Moe get? Line 10: What pet did Moe get?
6. Demonstrate understanding of syllable segmentation by clapping out syllables in words	Chunking Words	2–3 syllables: happy hamburger (3) jumping student's name	1–3 syllables: hamburger (3) excited (3) Moe student's name	2–4 syllables: excited (3) jumping pizza television (4)	2–4 syllables: hamburger (3) incredible (4) Moe student's name	2–4 syllables: happy excited television (4) teacher's name
7. Demonstrate understanding of phoneme segmentation by tapping out sounds in CVC words	Tapping Out Sounds					
8. Identify letter-sound correspondences	Letter Sounds Game	/**r**/, /s/, /a/, /m/	/r/, /s/, /a/, /m/	/**t**/, /r/, /s/, /a/, /m/	/t/, /r/, /s/, /a/, /m/	/t/, /r/, /s/, /a/, /m/

(Continued on next page)

Level 3 Scope and Sequence *(continued)*

Objective	Activity	Lesson 1	Lesson 2	Lesson 3	Lesson 4	Lesson 5
9. Point to and/or say the first/last sounds in words	First/Last Sound Game	sam, sat, tam, mat, rat	am, ram, mat, sat, tat	sat, rat, am, at, tat	mat, ram, sat, tam, at	sat, ran, mat, am, tam
10. Identify pictures that begin/end with given sounds	Finding Pictures with Special Sounds	sad, apple, milk, rose	rabbit, apple, man, soap	saw, tent, rake, mop	tooth, ring, man, ant	sun, rain, teeth, apple
11. Point to letter sounds in words	Stretching Words					
12. Blend sounds to identify pictures	Finding Pictures					
13. Point to pictures/words representing new vocabulary	The New Word Game	**dog, cat**	**snake,** dog	**rabbit,** cat	**bird,** rabbit	dog, bird
14. Use new vocabulary words and personal information to create a story	Fun with Writing	My pet is a ______.	My pet is not a snake. My pet is a ______.	My pet is not a rabbit. My pet is a ______.	My pet is not a bird. My pet is a ______.	My pet is a ______.

Lesson 1

Materials

- Moe the frog puppet
- Sight word flashcards: want, he, is, boy
- 2" × 2" Post-it® notes
- **Level 3 Student Response Book** (pages 148–177)
- Magnetic dry erase board and marker
- **All About Moe** easel book: "Moe Wants a Pet" story
- Pictures of pets
- Pencils, crayons, alphabetic rubber stamps, glue
- "My Book About Me" books completed by students in previous lessons
- "My Book About Me, My pet is a ______" page in Appendix D

Optional Materials

- AAC device
- Pointer/light pointer
- Plexiglas® for eye gazing
- Optional pictures or text for AAC device (see Appendix H):
  - Lesson Opening: Hello, Moe
  - Objective 4: pet
  - Objective 14: My pet is a ______.
  - Lesson Closing: Goodbye, Moe

Tips

- If needed, use the magnetic dry erase board and a marker (or magnetic objects) for reinforcement. Draw a line on the magnet board dividing it into two columns. At the top of the first column, place a picture of the student. At the top of the second column, place a picture of yourself. When a student responds appropriately, congratulate him or her for good work and place a mark on the student side. If a student does not respond appropriately, place a mark on your side. At the end of the lesson, count the marks and find out who had more for that day. Encourage students to participate by being enthusiastic about the marks they received.
- If a student requires an augmentative or alternative communication (AAC) device, preprogram it using the text from the optional materials list.
- All student materials (including AAC overlays and the "My Book About Me" pages) can be printed from Disc 1. Printing from the disc allows you to adapt the materials for students.
- If you are working with a student whose mode of responding is to eye-gaze, the student response options can be printed from Disc 1, laminated, and cut apart. The student choices can be adhered to Plexiglas® with Velcro®. Point to the correct answer after the student gazes to it to provide the watching peers with feedback.

▶ Lesson Opening

Engage the students by saying, **Good morning, Moe! Moe has been waiting for you. Moe is looking really excited this morning. I think he has something to tell you. Why don't you tell them, Moe?** Have Moe whisper in your ear. **OK, Moe. Moe is so excited, he can hardly talk. He wants you to know that he is going to a special place. And . . . he says that we will find out where he is going when we read the story today. First, let's practice our flashcard words so we can read the story. Then we will find out where Moe is going.** Have students use an AAC device if needed to say, "Hello, Moe."

Objective 1

Read sight words using time-delay instruction

Activity

Flashcard Game

Materials

- Moe the frog puppet
- Sight word flashcards: want, he, is, boy

Tip

A constant time-delay procedure is used to promote near-errorless responding. If a student is making errors in Round 1, which is the 0-second time-delay round, he or she may need additional practice (outside of this lesson) in imitating your model of choosing the correct response. Using pictures, have the student practice pointing where you point until he or she can do so fluently. If the student makes mistakes in Round 2, which is the 5-second time-delay round, shorten the time before you show the correct answer to 2 seconds. He or she will only have time to answer if certain. The student may also need to practice "wait training" to wait for the response. To do "wait training," use several sheets of different colored paper and say, **Point to the paper.** Have the student wait for you to point to show him or her which sheet.

Instructions

Flashcard Game: Part I. Part I of the Flashcard Game will give students practice saying or pointing to words with guidance.

Round 1: In this round, point to the correct answer as you ask the student to point (0-second time delay).

Lay the sight word flashcards in front of the students. Introduce the activity: **Let's play a game. I'll point to a word, then you point to the same word. Watch me.**

want	he
is	boy

Move the sight word flashcards in front of the first student. Point to the sight word ______ while saying, **This word is ______. (Student name), now you point to ______.**

Be sure you are pointing to the sight word as you say the word. Don't move your finger until the student points to where you are pointing. If you know a student will not imitate you, guide his or her hand for correct responding. For students who eye-gaze, use a light pointer or tap the answer to get them to focus their gaze on the correct answer.

When the student points to ______, say, **Yes, ______.** For students who are verbal, also say, **What word?** and have them say the word.

Wonderful job pointing to the word ______!

Shuffle the sight word flashcards and display them in a new order in front of the next student. In this round, each student takes a

turn pointing to the same sight word before moving on to the next sight word.

(Second student's name), point to ______. Be sure you are pointing to ______ as you say the word. Use the same prompt if required.

After each student's turn, shuffle the sight words around so they are not in the same position. Repeat shuffling sight words and pointing to the words until each student has had a turn with each word. Be sure all students are watching during each student's turn to encourage incidental learning.

Round 2: In Round 2 of the Flashcard Game, students point to or say the sight word independently. Moe is ready to help after giving the student up to 5 seconds to initiate a response (a 5-second time delay).

Have Moe whisper in your ear. **Okeydokey, Moe. We can do that. Moe wants you to find the word. He can help you if you are not sure. (Student's name), find the word _____.**

Allow the student 5 seconds to point to the word. After the student finds the word, have Moe point to the same word with the student. **(Student's name), you point with Moe. Thank you for helping, Moe.**

If the student is verbal, have him or her say the word also. If the student does not point, have Moe prompt the answer and restate the word.

Give each student a turn to practice pointing to the sight word you name. Shuffle the sight words and repeat the process for each student with the remaining words. Be sure all students are watching each other's turn.

Awesome playing the Flashcard Game! Moe is learning to read and so are you! Let's play the next game.

Assisting Students

Prompt If the student does not point to the word, use Moe to point to the correct word, saying, **Moe pointed to _____. Now you point to _____.** If the student still does not point, physically guide his or her hand.

Correction If the student points to the wrong word, model the correct response by pointing to the correct word and saying, **This is the word ______. Now you point to ______.** If the student still does not point to the correct word, physically guide his or her hand. Give a turn to another classmate, and praise that student for doing it correctly.

Pile on the Praise

Objective 2

Point to the sight words to complete sentences

Activity

Flashcard Game

Materials

- Moe the frog puppet
- Sight word flashcards: want, he, is, boy
- **Level 3 Student Response Book** (pages 148–155)

Instructions

Flashcard Game: Part II. Display the Student Response Book. Place Moe's mouth near your ear and appear to be intently listening. **Moe wants you to read your new word in a sentence. Moe, why do you need to read the words in sentences?** Place Moe's mouth near your ear again. **I see . . . that's what the "big frogs" do! The "big frogs" read words in sentences. Then that's what we want to do!**

Model reading sentence A.1 while pointing to each word in the sentence. Place verbal emphasis on the underlined word. **I really want a dog. Listen again. I really want a dog.**

Read sentence B.1, pointing to each word. **I really ______ a dog.** Point to the blank space.

Place the sight word flashcards in front of a student, using the correct answer and two distractors. **Show Moe which word goes here** (pointing back to the blank space in the sentence). **What word goes here? ______, ______, or ______?**

Allow the student 5 seconds to respond. If the student responds correctly, affirm by saying, **Yes, want. I really want a dog.**

Shuffle the sight words and repeat the script with sentences A.2 "**He is going to the pet store**" and B.2, as well as sentences A.3 "**Moe is excited**" and B.3, and A.4 "**The boy wants a snake**" and B.4.

Assisting Students

Prompt If the student does not respond within 5 seconds, read sentence A again, placing verbal emphasis on the sight word. Then read sentence B, pausing at the blank space.

______ is the word that goes here. I can find ______. Point to the correct sight word and say, **(Student's name), point to ______ with me. Yes, ______.**

Correction Do not allow students to practice incorrect responses. For a student who can point and is about to point to an incorrect response, physically guide his or her hand to the correct response while verbally reinforcing the response. For students who use eye-gaze and are visually attending to the incorrect response, remove the incorrect response and visually cue them to the correct response.

Objective 3

Point to text as it is read

Activity

Pointing to Words

Materials

- Moe the frog puppet
- "Moe Wants a Pet" story
- **Level 3 Student Response Book** (page 156)

Tips

- Use a wait time of 5 seconds for all responses in this activity. However, students may need longer than 5 seconds initially. In this case, responding within 5 seconds should be viewed as a goal to work toward. Note and track response time for any student for whom you feel it is physically difficult to respond within 5 seconds.
- The goal of text pointing in this level is to have students move left-to-right and top-to-bottom.
- Do not slow your speed of reading to accommodate students' speed of movement. Work toward having students keep pace with your speed of reading as they point to the text.

Instructions

Introduce the activity by saying, **Today we are going to read the story "Moe Wants a Pet."**

While displaying the easel book so all can see, read "Moe Wants a Pet" with enthusiasm, pointing to the text, moving left-to-right and top-to-bottom while you read.

After reading the story, return to the text-pointing page. Say, **Now Moe needs help reading his story. You can help him. I want you to point to each word in the line that I read. Like this.** While displaying the book so all can see, read lines 1–3 of "Moe Wants a Pet." Point to each word in lines 1–3 as you read. Then choose a student to point. Students can point to the text in the story, or you can use the page in the Student Response Book.

(Student's name), your turn! Point to the words for Moe as I read the line. I'm going to show you where to start, and I want you to follow along by pointing to each word as I read it. Show the student where to start pointing by touching the first word.

Repeat for each student, using the lines in the book (or in the Student Response Book).

Let's find out what Moe wants to do next!

Assisting Students

Prompt Modeling for the correct response is already built into the script. A student is given 5 seconds to begin responding. If the student does not initiate a response within 5 seconds, provide a visual cue. A visual cue might be tapping the page in the book and modeling the pointing. If there is still no response within 5 seconds, physically guide the student's hand to point to the words.

Objective 4

Say and/or point to a word to complete a repeated story line

Activity

Hidden Words

Materials

- Moe the frog puppet
- "Moe Wants a Pet" story (prepare for this activity by adhering a Post-it® note to cover the word *pet* highlighted in yellow in story line 3)
- **Level 3 Student Response Book** (page 157)

Tips

- For students who eye-gaze, print the student page from Disc 1 and cut the choices apart. Place the choices a distance apart so that you can discriminate the students' purposeful choices.
- If a student is unable to verbalize, program the AAC device to say the hidden word. Let the student activate the AAC device to say the hidden word and to choose the picture representing the hidden word.

Instructions

Have Moe whisper to you. **Let's play the Hidden Words game! I am going to read a line from the "Moe Wants a Pet" story, and I will point to a word that is hidden** (covered with the Post-it® note). **Get ready!**

Read lines 1 and 2 from "Moe Wants a Pet," emphasizing the word *pet* in line 2.

Read line 3, pausing to remove the Post-it® note. Point to the word *pet* and say, **Pet.**

Again cover the word *pet* in line 3. Say, **It's your turn, boys and girls! I am going to read these lines, and this time I want you (or a student's name) to say the hidden word. Get ready!**

Read lines 1–3, pausing for a student to indicate the hidden word *pet* in line 3. Uncover the word when students say it. Repeat until all students have had a turn.

Now Moe wants you to point to the picture and the word that tells what the hidden word was. First Moe is going to show you how to do it, and then you will have a turn. I will read the lines again, and he will point to a picture that tells what the uncovered word is. He has three choices here.

Point to the pictures in the Student Response Book and tell the students what the three choices are. Read lines 1–3 again, pausing on line 3 for Moe to point to the picture/word representing *pet.* Encourage students to say the uncovered word (use an AAC device for nonverbal students). Repeat the sequence for each student.

Assisting Students

Prompt If there is no response within 5 seconds, provide the student with a visual cue. A visual cue might consist of tapping (or using a light pointer to point to) the correct response. Say the word as you give the visual cue. If there is still no response within 5 seconds, physically guide the student's hand to the correct response. Say the word as you give the physical cue.

Objective 5

Respond to literal questions about a story

Activity

Answering Questions

Materials

- Moe the frog puppet
- "Moe Wants a Pet" story
- **Level 3 Student Response Book** (pages 158–161)

Tips

- Each line is numbered in the story. In this activity, lines 1, 2, and 6 are appropriate places to ask questions. When reading "Moe Wants a Pet," stop to ask questions after viewing the cover and at lines 1, 2, and 6. You do not need to ask each student each question; rather, have students take turns answering the questions.
- For students who eye-gaze, print the student page from Disc 1 and cut the choices apart. Place the choices a distance apart so that you can discriminate the students' purposeful choices.

Instructions

Start by having Moe whisper to you. **Moe wants to hear his story again. But this time, I am going to ask you some questions about Moe. You are going to answer the questions by pointing to a picture. The answers are here.** Touch the page in the Student Response Book. **Get ready!**

Read the story "Moe Wants a Pet," stopping to ask the following questions at the end of the designated lines. After asking the question, point to and name the answer choices in the Student Response Book, and then ask the question again. Encourage students who are verbal to point to the correct response and to say the correct response.

Question 1 after viewing the cover: **What do you think this story is going to be about?**
Question 2 from Line 1: **Who is excited?**
Question 3 from Line 2: **What kind of store is Moe going to?**
Question 4 from Line 6: **What pet could Moe get?**

Assisting Students

Prompt If there is no response within 5 seconds, provide the student with a visual cue. For this skill, you might ask Moe to do the visual prompt (e.g., say, **Moe, can you help [student's name] find the answer?**). A visual cue might consist of having Moe tap the correct response. Say, **Moe has shown you the answer. Now I will read the question again, and you show me the answer.** Read the question a second time. If there is still no response within 5 seconds, physically guide the student's hand to the correct response. Say the word as you give the physical cue.

Correction Do not allow students to practice incorrect responses. For a student who can point and is about to point to an incorrect response, physically guide his or her hand to the correct response while verbally reinforcing the response. For students who use eye-gaze and are visually attending to the incorrect response, remove the incorrect response and visually cue them to the correct response.

Objective 6

Demonstrate understanding of syllable segmentation by clapping out syllables in words

Activity

Chunking Words

Materials

- Moe the frog puppet

Tip

A great deal of thought must be given to how a student who is physically challenged will demonstrate this skill. When providing physical cues, make sure the cue can be faded over time. In order for the cue to be faded, the movement you choose must be one the student can create independently (e.g., don't use clapping as a physical cue if the student is unable to clap independently). One way to determine the best movement for the student to use would be to turn on some music, demonstrate moving to the music, and then watch to see what body part the student is able to move independently.

Instructions

Place Moe's mouth near your ear and appear to be listening intently. **Moe is very shy. He says words in a funny way. He says the sounds in words very slowly. Sometimes it is hard to figure out what he means. Moe wants us to help him. He wants to say the word *happy*. Okeydokey, Moe, you say *happy*.** Listen with concern as Moe says the word *happy*.

Have Moe say, ***Ha...ppy,*** slowly dividing it into two syllables.

Moe said *happy* the slow way. He said *ha...ppy*. I think he is trying to tell us the syllables he hears in *ha...ppy*. Moe, say *happy* again, and we'll clap out the syllables.

Model clapping out the two syllables in the word *happy* as Moe says the word. Make certain that Moe says *happy* slowly, clearly dividing the syllables as he speaks.

Have Moe say, ***Ha...ppy.***

Let's say *happy* again slowly and clap out the syllables for Moe. I'll clap and you help me. *Ha...ppy.* Help me do that again, boys and girls. Repeat the script.

Have Moe whisper in your ear. **Moe wants to try again with more words. Moe, you choose the next word!**

Have Moe say, ***Ham...bur...ger.***

Repeat the above script using: **hamburger, jumping,** and a **student's name** that is two to three syllables in length.

Objective 8

Identify letter-sound correspondences

Activity

Letter Sounds Game

Materials

- Moe the frog puppet
- **Level 3 Student Response Book** (pages 162–164)

Tip

When *a* letter appears between two virgules (/ /), say the sound the letter makes rather than the letter name (e.g., /r/ means to make the sound the letter *r* says). Stretch the sound when multiple letters (e.g., /rrr/) appear within the virgules.

Instructions

Letter Sounds Game: Part I. Part I introduces the letter *r* and the sound *r* makes. Introduce the activity: **We are going to play the Letter Sounds Game. It's a fun game. Here we go.**

Touch below the *r* on the Sound Presentation page in the Student Response Book and say, **This letter says /rrr/. The letter *r* says /rrr/. Touch /rrr/ with me.** Be sure you are pointing below the *r* as you say the sound. Don't move your finger until the student points to where you are pointing. **Your turn. Touch /rrr/.** Give each student an opportunity to touch the *r*.

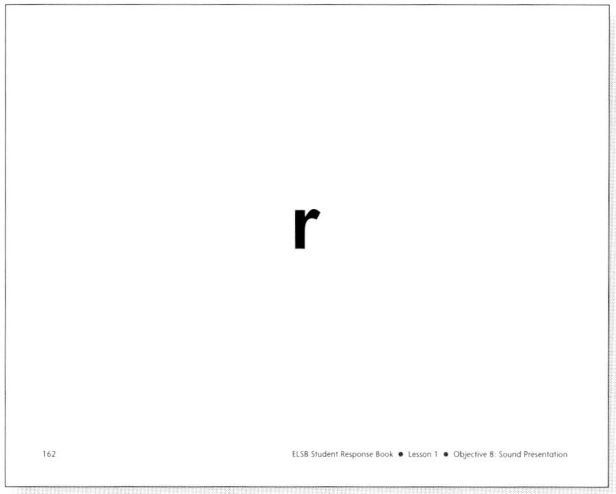

r

162 ELSB Student Response Book • Lesson 1 • Objective 8: Sound Presentation

Letter Sounds Game: Part II. Part II helps students discriminate the *r* sound from three distractors. Introduce the activity: **Now we get to do the next page of the Letter Sounds Game. Get ready!**

Turn to the Letter-Sound Discrimination page in the Student Response Book. **Touch /rrr/. Good job touching /rrr/. The letter *r* says /rrr/.** Give each student an opportunity to touch the *r*.

Whether students are verbal or nonverbal, encourage them to make the sound for *r*. **This time I will touch the *r* and you say the sound /rrr/. Ready?** Give each student an opportunity to say /r/.

For review, repeat the above script for the ***m, s,*** and ***a*** sounds.

Letter Sounds Game: Part III. Part III helps students identify and discriminate *r* when it is the beginning sound in words.

Turn to the Riley Rabbit page in the Student Response Book and say, **Our new sound is /rrr/. Let's practice. Touch /rrr/. Nice touching /rrr/. We are going to play a really fun game. First, we will listen to a poem called Riley the Real Rabbit. Riley loves**

_r_ words and foods that start with _r_. Let's read Riley's poem and see if we can hear words that start with /rrr/.

Read the following poem one time. While you read, point to the *r* on the Riley Rabbit page each time you say a word that begins with *r*.

Riley the Real Rabbit

Riley the **r**eal **r**abbit lives way down low,
way under the ground in a bunny **r**abbit hole.
Way under the ground where **r**eal **r**abbits go!

When **R**iley gets hungry, she comes out of the ground.
She looks for food.
She looks **r**ound and **r**ound.

Riley eats **r**aspberry leaves and **r**adish tops.
Then she **r**uns and jumps and plays and hops.

She hops over **r**ocks and **r**uns **r**ound and **r**ound.
Then **R**iley the **r**eal **r**abbit
runs back to the **r**abbit hole (which is under the ground)!

I will read the poem again and point to /rrr/ when I hear words that begin with /rrr/. This time you help me. You touch /rrr/ when you hear a word that starts with /rrr/.

Read the poem a second time and encourage students to listen and point to the *r* on the Riley Rabbit page when they hear words that begin with /r/. Stretch the beginning sound to emphasize the *r*. When a student touches the *r* at the appropriate time, give feedback and praise. For example: **Good. The first sound in _rabbit_ is /rrr/.** Note that students may find it difficult to point to the sound every time they hear it, but even pointing to the sound some of the time helps develop their phonemic awareness.

Assisting Students

Prompt If you know a student will not imitate you, guide his or her hand for correct responding. For students who eye-gaze, use a light pointer or tap the answer to get them to focus their gaze on the correct answer.

Correction Touch below the *r* and say, **This sound is /rrr/. Say /rrr/ with me. /rrr/. Say it by yourself. What sound?**

Objective 9

Point to and/or say the first/last sounds in words

Activity

First/Last Sound Game

Materials

- Moe the frog puppet
- **Level 3 Student Response Book** (page 165)

Tips

- When you say the word the "fast way," touch the colored smiley face to focus students, say "Ready," then slash under the word as you say it.
- Stretch the sound when multiple letters appear in the virgules (e.g., /sss/). Note that some sounds cannot be stretched (e.g., /t/).

Instructions

Place Moe's mouth near your ear and appear to be listening. **Moe wants us to get really good at knowing the first sounds in words. Moe has a fun game to play with colored smiling faces to help us hear the first sounds in words. OK, Moe! We are ready to play the First/Last Sound Game.**

Touch the green smiley face on the student page. **Get ready to read the word that comes after the green smiley face. I'll touch and say the first sound /sss/. I'll touch and say the next sound /aaa/. Then I will touch and say the last sound /mmm/. Say the sounds in this word with me: /sss/ /aaa/ /mmm/.**

I can say this word the fast way. Ready (put your finger on the smiley face, then say *sam* without segmenting it into sounds), ***sam*. Say this word the fast way with me, *sam*. Yes, *sam*. We said *sam* the fast way.**

Touch the first sound in *sam*. Say, **The first sound in *sam* is /sss/. Touch the first sound in *sam*.** Have a student touch or point to the *s*.

Say the first sound in *sam*. Place emphasis on the beginning sound when you say the word *sam*. **Yes, /sss/ is the first sound in the word *sam*.**

Repeat the script above for: **sat, tam, mat, rat,** changing the script to match the color of the smiley face and the beginning sound you are focusing on.

Assisting Students

Prompt If you know a student will not imitate you, guide his or her hand for correct responding. For students who eye-gaze, use a light pointer or tap the answer to get them to focus their gaze on the correct answer.

Correction Touch below each sound and say, **This sound is /_____/. Say /_____/ with me. /_____/. Say it by yourself. What sound?**

Objective 10

Identify pictures that begin/end with given sounds

Activity

Finding Pictures with Special Sounds

Materials

- Moe the frog puppet
- **Level 3 Student Response Book** (pages 166–169)

Instructions

Place Moe's mouth near your ear and appear to be listening. **Moe is ready to play his game. Finding Pictures with Special Sounds. The special sounds today are /sss/, /aaa/, /mmm/, and /rrr/.**

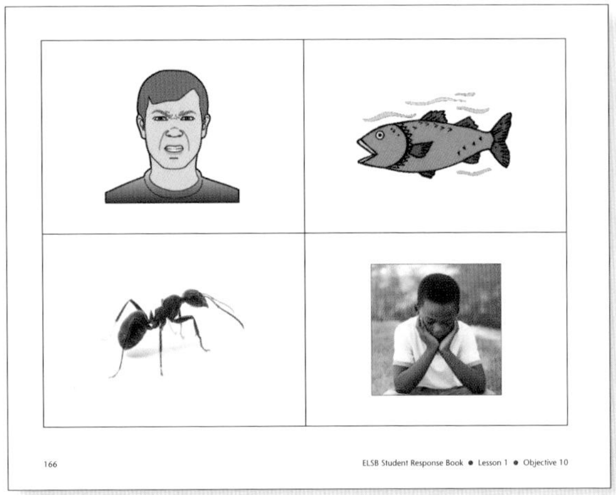

Display the Student Response Book. Point to each picture as you name it (mad, fish, ant, sad), placing emphasis on the first sound in each word.

Say the picture words with me.

The first sound in *mad* is /mmm/. The first sound in *fish* is /fff/. The first sound in *ant* is /aaa/. The first sound in *sad* is /sss/.

Point to the picture that has /sss/ as its first sound. Show me the picture that starts with /sss/.

Have a student point to the picture for sad. **Yes, the first sound in the word *sad* is /sss/.**

Repeat the above script for each student page. Change the script to match the target sound. The target response (focusing on either /a/, /m/, or /r/) has an asterisk in the list below.

girl, *apple, soap, fish
desk, leg, *milk, boy
***rose, pie, moon, sun**

Give all students 5 seconds to respond after you say, **Show me the picture that starts with ______.**

Assisting Students

Prompt and Correction

If there is no response within 5 seconds, point to the correct response and say, **The first sound in ______ is /_____/. Touch the picture of ______.** If the student does not respond within 5 seconds, physically guide the student's hand to the correct response and say, ______ **starts with /_____/.**

Objective 13

Point to pictures/words representing new vocabulary

Activity

The New Word Game

Materials

- Moe the frog puppet
- **Level 3 Student Response Book** (pages 170–177)

Instructions

Introduce the activity: **You are going to learn two new words to help you with your "My Book About Me" books. Your new words today are *dog* and *cat*.**

Open the Student Response Book and point to each picture for dog. Say, **This is a dog. And this is a dog. This is a dog, too.**

Give each student a turn to point to a picture of a dog. Say, **(Student's name), point to a dog.** If the student does not point, point to a picture and repeat the direction. If needed, physically guide the student's hand, saying, **This is a dog.**

Give each student a turn, pointing to a picture of a dog with each turn.

Turn to the next four student pages, which have a dog and three distractors, and say, **OK, I'm trying to trick you! Point to the picture of a dog.**

Give each student a turn. Use prompts as necessary.

Turn to the next three student pages and repeat the above script with: **cat.**

End the activity by saying, **Great job! Now let's use these words to write another page in your book.**

Assisting Students

Prompt If the student does not point to the picture, physically guide his or her hand, saying, **This is a dog (cat).**

Correction If the student points to the wrong picture, model pointing to the correct picture, saying, **This is a dog (cat). Now you point to a dog (cat).** If the student still does not point to the correct picture, physically guide his or her hand. Give a turn to another classmate, and praise that student for doing it correctly.

Objective 14

Use new vocabulary words and personal information to create a story

Activity

Fun with Writing

Materials

- "My Book About Me" books completed by students in previous lessons
- "My Book About Me, My pet is a ______" page in Appendix D
- Pencils, crayons, rubber alphabet stamps, glue
- Pictures of pets

Tips

- If a student is not able to write, have the student ask someone to write for him or her. If the student is not verbal, program an AAC device to state, "My pet is a ______." You can also create each student's pet response using a word processor and print in a size that will fit on the page. Students can also use the rubber alphabet stamps to stamp their responses.
- If the student is not able to read the sentences in their books, program an AAC device to read the sentences or to read the new sentence.
- If a student is not able to verbalize for the lesson closing, program an AAC device to say, "Goodbye, Moe."

Instructions

In this activity, students complete another page of their "My Book About Me" books by completing the following line:
My pet is a ______. Students can stamp their responses, write their responses with your assistance, or glue their responses (which have been prepared) on the line.

Introduce the activity: **Today you are going to write about a pet that you have or one you really want. Remember that you started making a book that was all about you! Now you can find your books.**

Lay out the "My Book About Me" books, asking students to identify their own. Review their book covers by reading the titles and pointing to the words as you read. Say, **Touch the first word at the top of the page, and read the name of this story with me. Remember, this story is all about you.**

Have each student point to the text as you read. Have students reread the pages of their books. Then present the pictures of pets.

Say, **Pick a picture of a pet that you have or would really like to have.**

Distribute the new "My Book About Me" page. Say, **Touch this sentence and read with me. My pet is a ______. Touch the pet that you have or the one that you want to have.** Help them glue the chosen picture at the end of the sentence. Then help them write their responses to complete the sentence about their pet, and add the page to their books. Read the sentences together.

Lesson Closing

Have Moe whisper in your ear. **Boys and girls, Moe said that you are too awesome! Moe will leave now, but he'll be back tomorrow! Say goodbye to Moe!** Have students say goodbye to Moe verbally or by using their AAC devices.

Lesson 2

Materials

- Moe the frog puppet
- Sight word flashcards: want, he, is, boy
- 2" × 2" Post-it® notes
- **Level 3 Student Response Book** (pages 178–207)
- Magnetic dry erase board and marker
- **All About Moe** easel book: "Moe Wants a Pet" story
- Pictures of pets
- Pictures of snakes
- Pencils, crayons, alphabetic rubber stamps, glue
- "My Book About Me" books completed by students in previous lessons
- "My Book About Me, My pet is not a snake. My pet is a ______" page in Appendix D

Optional Materials

- AAC device
- Pointer/light pointer
- Plexiglas® for eye gazing
- Optional pictures or text for AAC device (see Appendix H):
  - Lesson Opening: Good morning, Moe
  - Objective 4: dog
  - Objective 14: My pet is not a snake. My pet is a ______."
  - Lesson Closing: Goodbye, Moe

Tips

- If needed, use the magnetic dry erase board and a marker (or magnetic objects) for reinforcement. Draw a line on the magnet board dividing it into two columns. At the top of the first column, place a picture of the student. At the top of the second column, place a picture of yourself. When a student responds appropriately, congratulate him or her for good work and place a mark on the student side. If a student does not respond appropriately, place a mark on your side. At the end of the lesson, count the marks and find out who had more for that day. Encourage students to participate by being enthusiastic about the marks they received.
- If a student requires an augmentative or alternative communication (AAC) device, preprogram it using the text from the optional materials list.
- All student materials (including AAC overlays and the "My Book About Me" pages) can be printed from Disc 1. Printing from the disc allows you to adapt the materials for students.
- If you are working with a student whose mode of responding is to eye-gaze, the student response options can be printed from Disc 1, laminated, and cut apart. The student choices can be adhered to Plexiglas® with Velcro®. Point to the correct answer after the student gazes to it to provide the watching peers with feedback.

▶ Lesson Opening

Engage the students by saying, **Good morning, Moe! Moe has been waiting for you. Moe is looking really excited this morning. I think he has something to tell you. Why don't you tell them, Moe?** Have Moe whisper in your ear. **OK, Moe. Moe is so excited again, he can hardly talk. He wants you to know that he is going to a special place again. And . . . he says that we will find out where he is going when we read the story today. First, let's practice our flashcard words so we can read the story. Then we will find out where Moe is going.** Have students use an AAC device if needed to say, "Good morning, Moe."

Objective 1

Read sight words using time-delay instruction

Activity

Flashcard Game

Materials

- Moe the frog puppet
- Sight word flashcards: want, he, is, boy

Tip

A constant time-delay procedure is used to promote near-errorless responding. If a student is making errors in Round 1, which is the 0-second time-delay round, he or she may need additional practice (outside of this lesson) in imitating your model of choosing the correct response. Using pictures, have the student practice pointing where you point until he or she can do so fluently. If the student makes mistakes in Round 2, which is the 5-second time-delay round, shorten the time before you show the correct answer to 2 seconds. He or she will only have time to answer if certain. The student may also need to practice "wait training" to wait for the response. To do "wait training," use several sheets of different colored paper and say, **Point to the paper.** Have the student wait for you to point to show him or her which sheet.

Instructions

Flashcard Game: Part I. Part I of the Flashcard Game will give students practice saying or pointing to words with guidance.

Round 1: In this round, point to the correct answer as you ask the student to point (0-second time delay).

Lay the sight word flashcards in front of the students. Introduce the activity: **Let's play a game. I'll point to a word, then you point to the same word. Watch me.**

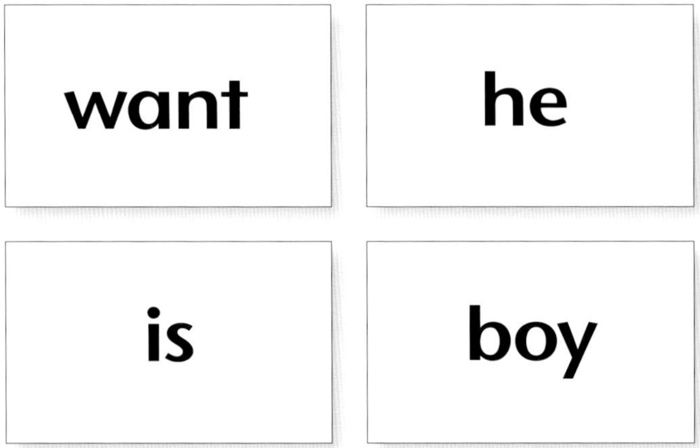

Move the sight word flashcards in front of the first student. Point to the sight word ______ while saying, **This word is ______. (Student name), now you point to ______.**

Be sure you are pointing to the sight word as you say the word. Don't move your finger until the student points to where you are pointing. If you know a student will not imitate you, guide his or her hand for correct responding. For students who eye-gaze, use a light pointer or tap the answer to get them to focus their gaze on the correct answer.

When the student points to _____, say, **Yes, _____.** For students who are verbal, also say, **What word?** and have them say the word.

Wonderful job pointing to the word _____!

Shuffle the sight word flashcards and display them in a new order in front of the next student. In this round, each student takes a turn pointing to the same sight word before moving on to the next sight word.

(Second student's name), point to _____. Be sure you are pointing to _____ as you say the word. Use the same prompt if required.

After each student's turn, shuffle the sight words around so they are not in the same position. Repeat shuffling sight words and pointing to the words until each student has had a turn with each word. Be sure all students are watching during each student's turn to encourage incidental learning.

Round 2: In Round 2 of the Flashcard Game, students point to or say the sight word independently. Moe is ready to help after giving the student up to 5 seconds to initiate a response (a 5-second time delay).

Have Moe whisper in your ear. **Okeydokey, Moe. We can do that. Moe wants you to find the word. He can help you if you are not sure. (Student's name), find the word _____.**

Allow the student 5 seconds to point to the word. After the student finds the word, have Moe point to the same word with the student. **(Student's name), you point with Moe. Thank you for helping, Moe.**

If the student is verbal, have him or her say the word also. If the student does not point, have Moe prompt the answer and restate the word.

Give each student a turn to practice pointing to the sight word you name. Shuffle the sight words and repeat the process for each student with the remaining words. Be sure all students are watching each other's turn.

Awesome playing the Flashcard Game! Moe is learning to read and so are you! Let's play the next game.

Assisting Students

Prompt If the student does not point to the word, use Moe to point to the correct word, saying, **Moe pointed to _____. Now you point to _____.** If the student still does not point, physically guide his or her hand.

Correction If the student points to the wrong word, model the correct response by pointing to the correct word and saying, **This is the word _____. Now you point to _____.** If the student still does not point to the correct word, physically guide his or her hand. Give a turn to another classmate, and praise that student for doing it correctly.

Pile on the Praise

Objective 2

Point to the sight words to complete sentences

Activity

Flashcard Game

Materials

- Moe the frog puppet
- Sight word flashcards: want, he, is, boy
- **Level 3 Student Response Book** (pages 178–185)

Instructions

Flashcard Game: Part II. Display the Student Response Book. Place Moe's mouth near your ear and appear to be intently listening. **Moe wants you to read your new word in a sentence. Moe, why do you need to read the words in sentences?** Place Moe's mouth near your ear again. **I see . . . that's what the "big frogs" do! The "big frogs" read words in sentences. Then that's what we want to do!**

Model reading sentence A.1 while pointing to each word in the sentence. Place verbal emphasis on the underlined word. **I want a bird. Listen again. I want a bird.**

Read sentence B.1, pointing to each word. **I ______ a bird.** Point to the blank space.

Place the sight word flashcards in front of a student, using the correct answer and two distractors. **Show Moe which word goes here** (pointing back to the blank space in the sentence). **What word goes here? ______, ______, or ______?**

Allow the student 5 seconds to respond. If the student responds correctly, affirm by saying, **Yes, want. I want a bird.**

Shuffle the sight words and repeat the script with sentences A.2 "**Moe doesn't know which pet he wants**" and B.2, as well as sentences A.3 "**The rabbit is soft**" and B.3, and A.4 "**The boy found a turtle**" and B.4.

Assisting Students

Prompt If the student does not respond within 5 seconds, read sentence A again, placing verbal emphasis on the sight word. Then read sentence B, pausing at the blank space.

______ is the word that goes here. I can find ______. Point to the correct sight word and say, **(Student's name), point to ______ with me. Yes, ______.**

Correction Do not allow students to practice incorrect responses. For a student who can point and is about to point to an incorrect response, physically guide his or her hand to the correct response while verbally reinforcing the response. For students who use eye-gaze and are visually attending to the incorrect response, remove the incorrect response and visually cue them to the correct response.

Objective 3

Point to text as it is read

Activity

Pointing to Words

Materials

- Moe the frog puppet
- "Moe Wants a Pet" story
- **Level 3 Student Response Book** (page 186)

Tips

- Use a wait time of 5 seconds for all responses in this activity. However, students may need longer than 5 seconds initially. In this case, responding within 5 seconds should be viewed as a goal to work toward. Note and track response time for any student for whom you feel it is physically difficult to respond within 5 seconds.
- The goal of text pointing in this level is to have students move left-to-right and top-to-bottom.
- Do not slow your speed of reading to accommodate students' speed of movement. Work toward having students keep pace with your speed of reading as they point to the text.

Instructions

Introduce the activity by saying, **Today we are going to read the story "Moe Wants a Pet."**

While displaying the easel book so all can see, read "Moe Wants a Pet" with enthusiasm, pointing to the text, moving left-to-right and top-to-bottom while you read.

After reading the story, return to the text-pointing page. Say, **Now Moe needs help reading his story. You can help him. I want you to point to each word in the line that I read. Like this.** While displaying the book so all can see, read lines 6–8 of "Moe Wants a Pet." Point to each word in lines 6–8 as you read. Then choose a student to point. Students can point to the text in the story, or you can use the page in the Student Response Book.

(Student's name), your turn! Point to the words for Moe as I read the line. I'm going to show you where to start, and I want you to follow along by pointing to each word as I read it. Show the student where to start pointing by touching the first word.

Repeat for each student, using the lines in the book (or in the Student Response Book).

Let's find out what Moe wants to do next!

Assisting Students

Prompt Modeling for the correct response is already built into the script. A student is given 5 seconds to begin responding. If the student does not initiate a response within 5 seconds, provide a visual cue. A visual cue might be tapping the page in the book and modeling the pointing. If there is still no response within 5 seconds, physically guide the student's hand to point to the words.

Objective 4

Say and/or point to a word to complete a repeated story line

Activity

Hidden Words

Materials

- Moe the frog puppet
- "Moe Wants a Pet" story (prepare for this activity by adhering a Post-it® note to cover the word *dog* highlighted in yellow in story line 11)
- **Level 3 Student Response Book** (page 187)

Tips

- For students who eye-gaze, print the student page from Disc 1 and cut the choices apart. Place the choices a distance apart so that you can discriminate the students' purposeful choices.

- If a student is unable to verbalize, program the AAC device to say the hidden word. Let the student activate the AAC device to say the hidden word and to choose the picture representing the hidden word.

Instructions

Have Moe whisper to you. **Let's play the Hidden Words game! I am going to read a line from the "Moe Wants a Pet" story, and I will point to a word that is hidden** (covered with the Post-it® note). **Get ready!**

Read lines 9 and 10 from "Moe Wants a Pet," emphasizing the word *dog.*

Read line 11, pausing to remove the Post-it® note. Point to the word *dog* and say, **Dog.**

Again cover the word *dog* in line 11. Say, **It's your turn, boys and girls! I am going to read these lines, and this time I want you (or a student's name) to say the hidden word. Get ready!**

Read lines 9–11, pausing for a student to indicate the hidden word *dog* in line 11. Repeat until all students have had a turn.

Now Moe wants you to point to the picture and the word that tells what the hidden word was. First Moe is going to show you how to do it, and then you will have a turn. I will read the lines again, and he will point to a picture that tells what the uncovered word is. He has three choices here.

Point to the pictures in the Student Response Book and tell the students what the three choices are. Read lines 9–11 again, pausing on line 11 for Moe to point to the picture/word representing *dog.* Encourage students to say the uncovered word (use an AAC device for nonverbal students). Repeat the sequence for each student.

Assisting Students

Prompt If there is no response within 5 seconds, provide the student with a visual cue. A visual cue might consist of tapping (or using a light pointer to point to) the correct response. Say the word as you give the visual cue. If there is still no response within 5 seconds, physically guide the student's hand to the correct response. Say the word as you give the physical cue.

Objective 5

Respond to literal questions about a story

Activity

Answering Questions

Materials

- Moe the frog puppet
- "Moe Wants a Pet" story
- **Level 3 Student Response Book** (pages 188–191)

Tips

- Each line is numbered in the story. In this activity, lines 1, 2, and 9 are appropriate places to ask questions. When reading "Moe Wants a Pet," stop to ask questions after reading lines 1, 2, and 9, and at the end of the story. You do not need to ask each student each question; rather, have students take turns answering the questions.
- For students who eye-gaze, print the student page from Disc 1 and cut the choices apart. Place the choices a distance apart so that you can discriminate the students' purposeful choices.

Instructions

Start by having Moe whisper to you. **Moe wants to hear his story again. But this time, I am going to ask you some questions about Moe. You are going to answer the questions by pointing to a picture. The answers are here.** Touch the page in the Student Response Book. **Get ready!**

Read the story "Moe Wants a Pet," stopping to ask the following questions at the end of the designated lines. After asking the question, point to and name the answer choices in the Student Response Book, and then ask the question again. Encourage students who are verbal to point to the correct response and to say the correct response.

Question 1 from Line 1: **How does Moe feel?**
Question 2 from Line 2: **How many pets can Moe get?**
Question 3 from Line 9: **Does Moe want a cat, a dog, or a goat?**
Question 4 after reading the entire story: **What was the story about?**

Assisting Students

Prompt If there is no response within 5 seconds, provide the student with a visual cue. For this skill, you might ask Moe to do the visual prompt (e.g., say, **Moe, can you help [student's name] find the answer?**). A visual cue might consist of having Moe tap the correct response. Say, **Moe has shown you the answer. Now I will read the question again, and you show me the answer.** Read the question a second time. If there is still no response within 5 seconds, physically guide the student's hand to the correct response. Say the word as you give the physical cue.

Correction Do not allow students to practice incorrect responses. For a student who can point and is about to point to an incorrect response, physically guide his or her hand to the correct response while verbally reinforcing the response. For students who use eye-gaze and are visually attending to the incorrect response, remove the incorrect response and visually cue them to the correct response.

Objective 6

Demonstrate understanding of syllable segmentation by clapping out syllables in words

Activity

Chunking Words

Materials

- Moe the frog puppet

Tip

A great deal of thought must be given to how a student who is physically challenged will demonstrate this skill. When providing physical cues, make sure the cue can be faded over time. In order for the cue to be faded, the movement you choose must be one the student can create independently (e.g., don't use clapping as a physical cue if the student is unable to clap independently). One way to determine the best movement for the student to use would be to turn on some music, demonstrate moving to the music, and then watch to see what body part the student is able to move independently.

Instructions

Place Moe's mouth near your ear and appear to be listening intently. **Remember, Moe is very shy. He says words in a funny way. He says the sounds in words very slowly. Sometimes it is hard to figure out what he means. Moe wants us to help him. He wants to say the word *hamburger.* Okeydokey, Moe, you say *hamburger.*** Listen with concern as Moe says the word *hamburger.*

Have Moe say, ***Ham...bur...ger,*** slowly dividing it into three syllables.

Moe said *hamburger* the slow way. He said *ham...bur...ger.* I think he is trying to tell us the syllables he hears in *ham...bur...ger.* Moe, say *hamburger* again, and we'll clap out the syllables.

Model clapping out the three syllables in the word *hamburger* as Moe says the word. Make certain that Moe says *hamburger* slowly, clearly dividing the syllables as he speaks.

Have Moe say, ***Ham...bur...ger.***

Let's say *hamburger* again slowly and clap out the syllables for Moe. I'll clap and you help me. *Ham...bur...ger.* Help me do that again, boys and girls. Repeat the script.

Have Moe whisper in your ear. **Moe wants to try again with more words. Moe, you choose the next word!**

Have Moe say, ***Ex...ci...ted.***

Repeat the above script using **excited, Moe,** and a **student's name** that is two to three syllables in length.

Objective 8

Identify letter-sound correspondences

Activity

Letter Sounds Game

Materials

- Moe the frog puppet
- **Level 3 Student Response Book** (pages 192–194)

Tip

When a letter appears between two virgules (/ /), say the sound the letter makes rather than the letter name (e.g., /r/ means to make the sound the letter *r* says). Stretch the sound when multiple letters (e.g., /rrr/) appear within the virgules.

Instructions

Letter Sounds Game: Part I. Part I reviews the letter *r* and the sound *r* makes. Introduce the activity: **We are going to play the Letter Sounds Game. It's a fun game. Here we go.**

Touch below the *r* on the Sound Presentation page in the Student Response Book and say, **This letter says /rrr/. This letter *r* says /rrr/. Touch /rrr/ with me.** Be sure you are pointing below the *r* as you say the sound. Don't move your finger until the student points to where you are pointing. **Your turn. Touch /rrr/.** Give each student an opportunity to touch the *r*.

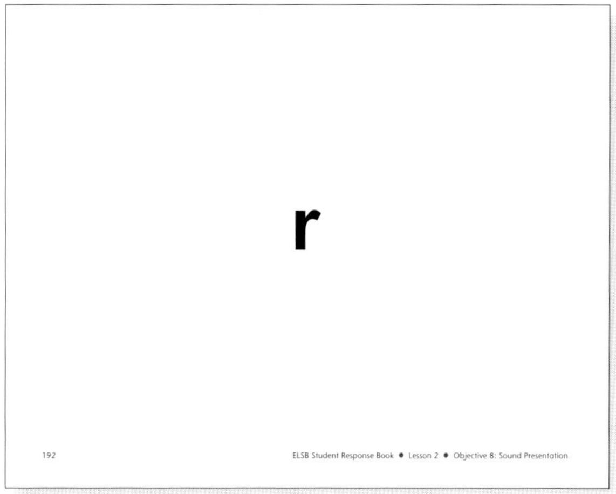
r

192 ELSB Student Response Book • Lesson 2 • Objective 8: Sound Presentation

Letter Sounds Game: Part II. Part II helps students discriminate the *r* sound from three distractors. Introduce the activity: **Now we get to do the next page of the Letter Sounds Game. Get ready!**

Turn to the Letter-Sound Discrimination page in the Student Response Book. **Touch /rrr/. Good job touching /rrr/. The letter *r* says /rrr/.** Give each student an opportunity to touch the *r*.

Whether students are verbal or nonverbal, encourage them to make the sound for *r*. **This time I will touch the *r* and you say the sound /rrr/. Ready?** Give each student an opportunity to say /r/.

For review, repeat the above script for the other letters on the page.

Letter Sounds Game: Part III. Part III helps students identify and discriminate *r* when it is the beginning sound in words.

Turn to the Riley Rabbit page in the Student Response Book and say, **Our new sound is /rrr/. Let's practice. Touch /rrr/. Nice touching /rrr/. We are going to play a really fun game. First, we will listen to the poem called Riley the Real Rabbit.**

Remember, Riley loves *r* words and foods that start with *r*. Let's read Riley's poem and see if we can hear words that start with /rrr/.

Read the following poem one time. While you read, point to the *r* on the Riley Rabbit page each time you say a word that begins with *r*.

Riley the Real Rabbit

Riley the **r**eal **r**abbit lives way down low,
way under the ground in a bunny **r**abbit hole.
Way under the ground where **r**eal **r**abbits go!

When **R**iley gets hungry, she comes out of the ground.
She looks for food.
She looks **r**ound and **r**ound.

Riley eats **r**aspberry leaves and **r**adish tops.
Then she **r**uns and jumps and plays and hops.

She hops over **r**ocks and **r**uns **r**ound and **r**ound.
Then **R**iley the **r**eal **r**abbit
runs back to the **r**abbit hole (which is under the ground)!

I will read the poem again and point to /rrr/ when I hear words that begin with /rrr/. This time you help me. You touch /rrr/ when you hear a word that starts with /rrr/.

Read the poem a second time and encourage students to listen and point to the *r* on the Riley Rabbit page when they hear words that begin with /r/. Stretch the beginning sound to emphasize the *r*. When a student touches the *r* at the appropriate time, give feedback and praise. For example: **Good. The first sound in *rabbit* is /rrr/.** Note that students may find it difficult to point to the sound every time they hear it, but even pointing to the sound some of the time helps develop their phonemic awareness.

Assisting Students

Prompt If you know a student will not imitate you, guide his or her hand for correct responding. For students who eye-gaze, use a light pointer or tap the answer to get them to focus their gaze on the correct answer.

Correction Touch below the *r* and say, **This sound is /rrr/. Say /rrr/ with me. /rrr/. Say it by yourself. What sound?**

Objective 9

Point to and/or say the first/last sounds in words

Activity

First/Last Sound Game

Materials

- Moe the frog puppet
- **Level 3 Student Response Book** (page 195)

Tips

- When you say the word the "fast way," touch the colored smiley face to focus students, say "Ready," then slash under the word as you say it.
- Stretch the sound when multiple letters appear in the virgules (e.g., /sss/). Note that some sounds cannot be stretched (e.g., /t/).

Instructions

Place Moe's mouth near your ear and appear to be listening. **Moe wants us to get really good at knowing the first sounds in words. Moe has a fun game to play with colored smiling faces to help us hear the first sounds in words. OK, Moe! We are ready to play the First/Last Sound Game.**

Touch the green smiley face on the student page. **Get ready to read the word that comes after the green smiley face. I'll touch and say the first sound /aaa/. Then I will touch and say the last sound /m/.**

Say the sounds in this word with me: /aaa/ /mmm/.

I can say this word the fast way. Ready (put your finger on the smiley face, then say am without segmenting it into sounds), ***am*. Say this word the fast way with me, *am*. Yes, *am*. We said *am* the fast way.**

Touch the first sound in *am*. Say, **The first sound in *am* is /aaa/. Touch the first sound in *am*.** Have a student touch or point to the *a*.

Say the first sound in *am*. Place emphasis on the beginning sound when you say the word *am*. **Yes, /aaa/ is the first sound in the word *am*.**

Repeat the script above for: **ram, mat, sat, tat,** changing the script to match the color of the smiley face and the beginning sound you are focusing on.

Assisting Students

Prompt If you know a student will not imitate you, guide his or her hand for correct responding. For students who eye-gaze, use a light pointer or tap the answer to get them to focus their gaze on the correct answer.

Correction Touch below each sound and say, **This sound is /_____/. Say /_____/ with me. /_____/. Say it by yourself. What sound?**

Objective 10

Identify pictures that begin/end with given sounds

Activity

Finding Pictures with Special Sounds

Materials

- Moe the frog puppet
- **Level 3 Student Response Book** (pages 196–199)

Instructions

Place Moe's mouth near your ear and appear to be listening. **Moe is ready to play his game: Finding Pictures with Special Sounds. The special sounds today are /rrr/, /aaa/, /mmm/, and /sss/.**

Display the Student Response Book. Point to each picture as you name it (fan, rabbit, mouse, sock), placing emphasis on the first sound in each word.

Say the picture words with me. The first sound in *fan* is /fff/. The first sound in *rabbit* is /rrr/. /The first sound in *mouse* is /mmm/. The first sound in *sock* is /sss/.

Point to the picture that has /rrr/ as its first sound. Show me the picture that starts with /rrr/.

Have a student point to the rabbit. **Yes, the first sound in the word *rabbit* is /rrr/.**

Repeat the above script for each student page. Change the script to match the target sound. The target response (focusing on either /a/, /m/, or /s/) has an asterisk in the list below.

***apple, moon, sink, vase**
book, sun, fence, *man
lake, fire, *soap, ball

Give all students 5 seconds to respond after you say, **Show me the picture that starts with ______.**

Assisting Students

Prompt and Correction

If there is no response within 5 seconds, point to the correct response and say, **The first sound in ______ is /_____/. Touch the picture of ______.** If the student does not respond within 5 seconds, physically guide the student's hand to the correct response and say, ______ **starts with /_____/.**

Objective 13

Point to pictures representing new vocabulary

Activity

The New Word Game

Materials

- Moe the frog puppet
- **Level 3 Student Response Book** (pages 200–207)

Instructions

Introduce the activity: **Today we are going to talk about a new word and a word you already know. Your new word is *snake.* The other word is *dog.***

Open the Student Response Book and point to each picture of a snake. Say, **This is a snake. This is a snake. And this is a snake.**

Give each student a turn to point to a picture of a snake. Say, **(Student's name), point to a snake.** If the student does not point, point to a picture and repeat the direction. If needed, physically guide the student's hand, saying, **This is a snake.**

Give each student a turn, pointing to a picture of a snake with each turn.

Turn to the next three student pages, which have a snake and three distractors, and say, **OK, I'm trying to trick you! Point to the picture of a snake.**

Give each student a turn. Use prompts as necessary.

Turn to the next four student pages and repeat the above script with: **dog.**

End the activity by saying, **Great job! Now let's use these words to write another page in your book.**

Assisting Students

Prompt If the student does not point to the picture, physically guide his or her hand, saying, **This is a snake (dog).**

Correction If the student points to the wrong picture, model pointing to the correct picture, saying, **This is a snake (dog). Now you point to a snake (dog).** If the student still does not point to the correct picture, physically guide his or her hand. Give a turn to another classmate, and praise that student for doing it correctly.

Objective 14

Use new vocabulary words and personal information to create a story

Activity

Fun with Writing

Materials

- "My Book About Me" books completed by students in previous lessons
- "My Book About Me, My pet is not a snake. My pet is a ______" page in Appendix D
- Pencils, crayons, rubber alphabet stamps, glue
- Pictures of pets
- Pictures of snakes

Tips

- If a student is not able to write, have the student ask someone to write for him or her. If the student is not verbal, program an AAC device to state, "My pet is not a snake. My pet is a ______." You can also create each student's pet response using a word processor and print in a size that will fit on the page. Students can also use the rubber alphabet stamps to stamp their responses.
- If the student is not able to read the sentences in their books, program an AAC device to read the sentences.
- If a student is not able to verbalize for the lesson closing, use an AAC device to say, "Goodbye, Moe."

Instructions

In this activity, students complete another page of their "My Book About Me" books by completing the following: My pet is not a snake. My pet is a ______. Students can stamp their responses, write their responses with your assistance, or glue their responses (which have been prepared) on the line.

Introduce the activity: Lay out the "My Book About Me" books, asking students to identify their own. Present the pictures of pets and snakes. Say, **Pick a picture of a pet that you have or would really like to have. Then pick a picture of a snake.**

Distribute the new "My Book About Me" page. Say, **Touch these sentences and read with me. My pet is not a snake. My pet is a ______. Touch the pet that you have or the one that you want to have.** Help them glue the chosen pet picture at the end of the sentence. Then help them write their responses to complete the sentence about their pet. Read the sentences together.

Help the students paste the picture of the chosen snake on the page. The students can use a red marker to place an *X* on the snake to show their pet is not a snake. Encourage all students to use a writing utensil to scribble, write, draw, etc., at the top of the page, and add the page to their books.

Lesson Closing

Have Moe whisper in your ear. **Boys and girls, Moe said you are incredible workers! Moe will leave now, but he'll be back tomorrow! Say goodbye to Moe!** Have students say goodbye to Moe verbally or by using their AAC devices.

Lesson 3

Materials

- Moe the frog puppet
- Sight word flashcards: want, he, is, boy
- 2" × 2" Post-it® notes
- **Level 3 Student Response Book** (pages 208–237)
- Magnetic dry erase board and marker
- **All About Moe** easel book: "Moe Gets a Pet" story
- Pictures of pets
- Pictures of rabbits
- Pencils, crayons, alphabetic rubber stamps, glue
- "My Book About Me" books completed by students in previous lessons
- "My Book About Me, My pet is not a rabbit. My pet is a ______" page in Appendix D

Optional Materials

- AAC device
- Pointer/light pointer
- Plexiglas® for eye gazing
- Optional pictures or text for AAC device (see Appendix H):
  - Lesson Opening: Hello, Moe
  - Objective 4: dog
  - Objective 14: My pet is not a rabbit. My pet is a ______.
  - Lesson Closing: Goodbye, Moe

Tips

- If needed, use the magnetic dry erase board and a marker (or magnetic objects) for reinforcement. Draw a line on the magnet board dividing it into two columns. At the top of the first column, place a picture of the student. At the top of the second column, place a picture of yourself. When a student responds appropriately, congratulate him or her for good work and place a mark on the student side. If a student does not respond appropriately, place a mark on your side. At the end of the lesson, count the marks and find out who had more for that day. Encourage students to participate by being enthusiastic about the marks they received.

- If a student requires an augmentative or alternative communication (AAC) device, preprogram it using the text from the optional materials list.

- All student materials (including AAC overlays and the "My Book About Me" pages) can be printed from Disc 1. Printing from the disc allows you to adapt the materials for students.

- If you are working with a student whose mode of responding is to eye-gaze, the student response options can be printed from Disc 1, laminated, and cut apart. The student choices can be adhered to Plexiglas® with Velcro®. Point to the correct answer after the student gazes to it to provide the watching peers with feedback.

▶ Lesson Opening

Engage the students by saying, **Good morning, Moe! Moe has been waiting for you. Moe is looking really excited this morning. I think he has something to tell you. Why don't you tell them, Moe?** Have Moe whisper in your ear. **OK, Moe. Moe is so excited again, he can hardly talk. He wants you to know that he is going to a special place again. And . . . he says that we will find out where he is going when we read the story today. First, let's practice our flashcard words so we can read the story. Then we will find out where Moe is going.** Have students use an AAC device if needed to say, "Hello, Moe."

Objective 1

Read sight words using time-delay instruction

Activity

Flashcard Game

Materials

- Moe the frog puppet
- Sight word flashcards: want, he, is, boy

Tip

A constant time-delay procedure is used to promote near-errorless responding. If a student is making errors in Round 1, which is the 0-second time-delay round, he or she may need additional practice (outside of this lesson) in imitating your model of choosing the correct response. Using pictures, have the student practice pointing where you point until he or she can do so fluently. If the student makes mistakes in Round 2, which is the 5-second time-delay round, shorten the time before you show the correct answer to 2 seconds. He or she will only have time to answer if certain. The student may also need to practice "wait training" to wait for the response. To do "wait training," use several sheets of different colored paper and say, **Point to the paper.** Have the student wait for you to point to show him or her which sheet.

Instructions

Flashcard Game: Part I. Part I of the Flashcard Game will give students practice saying or pointing to words with guidance.

Round 1: In this round, point to the correct answer as you ask the student to point (0-second time delay).

Lay the sight word flashcards in front of the students. Introduce the activity: **Let's play a game. I'll point to a word, then you point to the same word. Watch me.**

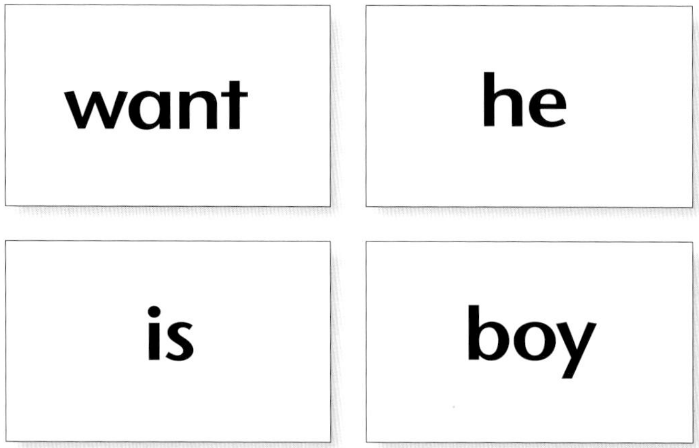

Move the sight word flashcards in front of the first student. Point to the sight word _____ while saying, **This word is _____. (Student name), now you point to ______.**

Be sure you are pointing to the sight word as you say the word. Don't move your finger until the student points to where you are pointing. If you know a student will not imitate you, guide his or her hand for correct responding. For students who eye-gaze, use a light pointer or tap the answer to get them to focus their gaze on the correct answer.

When the student points to ______, say, **Yes, ______.** For students who are verbal, also say, **What word?** and have them say the word.

Wonderful job pointing to the word ______!

Shuffle the sight word flashcards and display them in a new order in front of the next student. In this round, each student takes a

turn pointing to the same sight word before moving on to the next sight word.

(Second student's name), point to ______. Be sure you are pointing to ______ as you say the word. Use the same prompt if required.

After each student's turn, shuffle the sight words around so they are not in the same position. Repeat shuffling sight words and pointing to the words until each student has had a turn with each word. Be sure all students are watching during each student's turn to encourage incidental learning.

Round 2: In Round 2 of the of the Flashcard Game, students point to or say the sight word independently. Moe is ready to help after giving the student up to 5 seconds to initiate a response (a 5-second time delay).

Have Moe whisper in your ear. **Okeydokey, Moe. We can do that. Moe wants you to find the word. He can help you if you are not sure. (Student's name), find the word ______.**

Allow the student 5 seconds to point to the word. After the student finds the word, have Moe point to the same word with the student. **(Student's name), you point with Moe. Thank you for helping, Moe.**

If the student is verbal, have him or her say the word also. If the student does not point, have Moe prompt the answer and restate the word.

Give each student a turn to practice pointing to the sight word you name. Shuffle the sight words and repeat the process for each student with the remaining words. Be sure all students are watching each other's turn.

Awesome playing the Flashcard Game! Moe is learning to read and so are you! Let's play the next game.

Assisting Students

Prompt If the student does not point to the word, use Moe to point to the correct word, saying, **Moe pointed to _____. Now you point to _____.** If the student still does not point, physically guide his or her hand.

Correction If the student points to the wrong word, model the correct response by pointing to the correct word and saying, **This is the word ______. Now you point to ______.** If the student still does not point to the correct word, physically guide his or her hand. Give a turn to another classmate, and praise that student for doing it correctly.

Pile on the Praise

Objective 2

Point to the sight words to complete sentences

Activity

Flashcard Game

Materials

- Moe the frog puppet
- Sight word flashcards: want, he, is, boy
- **Level 3 Student Response Book** (pages 208–215)

Instructions

Flashcard Game: Part II. Display the Student Response Book. Place Moe's mouth near your ear and appear to be intently listening. **Moe wants you to read your new word in a sentence. Moe, why do you need to read the words in sentences?** Place Moe's mouth near your ear again. **I see . . . that's what the "big frogs" do! The "big frogs" read words in sentences. Then that's what we want to do!**

Model reading sentence A.1 while pointing to each word in the sentence. Place verbal emphasis on the underlined word. **How much do you want? Listen again. How much do you want?**

Read sentence B.1, pointing to each word. **How much do you ______?** Point to the blank space.

Place the sight word flashcards in front of a student, using the correct answer and two distractors. **Show Moe which word goes here** (pointing back to the blank space in the sentence). **What word goes here? ______, ______, or ______?**

Allow the student 5 seconds to respond. If the student responds correctly, affirm by saying, **Yes, want. How much do you want?**

Shuffle the sight words and repeat the script with sentences A.2 "**First he saw a dog**" and B.2, as well as sentences A.3 "**Moe is a frog**" and B.3, and A.4 "**Jason is a boy**" and B.4.

Assisting Students

Prompt If the student does not respond within 5 seconds, read sentence A again, placing verbal emphasis on the sight word. Then read sentence B, pausing at the blank space.

______ is the word that goes here. I can find ______. Point to the correct sight word and say, **(Student's name), point to ______ with me. Yes, ______.**

Correction Do not allow students to practice incorrect responses. For a student who can point and is about to point to an incorrect response, physically guide his or her hand to the correct response while verbally reinforcing the response. For students who use eye-gaze and are visually attending to the incorrect response, remove the incorrect response and visually cue them to the correct response.

Objective 3

Point to text as it is read

Activity

Pointing to Words

Materials

- Moe the frog puppet
- "Moe Gets a Pet" story
- **Level 3 Student Response Book** (page 216)

Tips

- Use a wait time of 5 seconds for all responses in this activity. However, students may need longer than 5 seconds initially. In this case, responding within 5 seconds should be viewed as a goal to work toward. Note and track response time for any student for whom you feel it is physically difficult to respond within 5 seconds.
- The goal of text pointing in this level is to have students move left-to-right and top-to-bottom.
- Do not slow your speed of reading to accommodate students' speed of movement. Work toward having students keep pace with your speed of reading as they point to the text.

Instructions

Introduce the activity by saying, **Today we are going to read the story "Moe Gets a Pet."**

While displaying the easel book so all can see, read "Moe Gets a Pet" with enthusiasm, pointing to the text, moving left-to-right and top-to-bottom while you read.

After reading the story, return to the text-pointing page. Say, **Now Moe needs help reading his story. You can help him. I want you to point to each word in the line that I read. Like this.** While displaying the book so all can see, read lines 1–3 of "Moe Gets a Pet." Point to each word in lines 1–3 as you read. Then choose a student to point. Students can point to the text in the story, or you can use the page in the Student Response Book.

(Student's name), your turn! Point to the words for Moe as I read the line. I'm going to show you where to start, and I want you to follow along by pointing to each word as I read it. Show the student where to start pointing by touching the first word.

Repeat for each student, using the lines in the book (or in the Student Response Book).

Let's find out what Moe wants to do next!

Assisting Students

Prompt Modeling for the correct response is already built into the script. A student is given 5 seconds to begin responding. If the student does not initiate a response within 5 seconds, provide a visual cue. A visual cue may be tapping the page in the book and modeling the pointing. If there is still no response within 5 seconds, physically guide the student's hand to point to the words.

Objective 4

Say and/or point to a word to complete a repeated story line

Activity

Hidden Words

Materials

- Moe the frog puppet
- "Moe Gets a Pet" story (prepare for this activity by adhering a Post-it® note to cover the word *dog* highlighted in yellow in story line 4)
- **Level 3 Student Response Book** (page 217)

Tips

- For students who eye-gaze, print the student page from Disc 1 and cut the choices apart. Place the choices a distance apart so that you can discriminate the students' purposeful choices.
- If a student is unable to verbalize, program the AAC device to say the hidden word. Let the student activate the AAC device to say the hidden word and to choose the picture representing the hidden word.

Instructions

Have Moe whisper to you. **Let's play the Hidden Words game! I am going to read a line from the "Moe Gets a Pet" story, and I will point to a word that is hidden** (covered with the Post-it® note). **Get ready!**

Read line 3 from "Moe Gets a Pet," emphasizing the word *dog*.

Read line 4, pausing to remove the Post-it® note. Point to the word *dog* and say, **Dog.**

Again cover the word dog in line 4. Say, **It's your turn, boys and girls! I am going to read these lines and this time I want you (or a student's name) to say the hidden word. Get ready!**

Read lines 3 and 4, pausing for a student to indicate the hidden word *dog* in line 4. Uncover the word when students say it. Repeat until all students have had a turn.

Now Moe wants you to point to the picture and the word that tells what the hidden word was. First Moe is going to show you how to do it and then you will have a turn. I will read the lines again, and he will point to a picture that tells what the uncovered word is. He has three choices here.

Point to the pictures in the Student Response Book and tell the students what the three choices are. Read lines 3 and 4 again, pausing on line 4 for Moe to point to the picture/word representing *dog*. Encourage students to say the uncovered word (use an AAC device for nonverbal students). Repeat the sequence for each student.

Assisting Students

Prompt If there is no response within 5 seconds, provide the student with a visual cue. A visual cue might consist of tapping (or using a light pointer to point to) the correct response. Say the word as you give the visual cue. If there is still no response within 5 seconds, physically guide the student's hand to the correct response. Say the word as you give the physical cue.

Objective 5

Respond to literal questions about a story

Activity

Answering Questions

Materials

- Moe the frog puppet
- "Moe Gets a Pet" story
- **Level 3 Student Response Book** (pages 218–221)

Tips

- Each line is numbered in the story. In this activity, lines 1, 3, and 10 are appropriate places to ask questions. When reading "Moe Gets a Pet," stop to ask questions after viewing the cover and after reading lines 1, 3, and 10. You do not need to ask each student each question; rather, have students take turns answering the questions.
- For students who eye-gaze, print the student page from Disc 1 and cut the choices apart. Place the choices a distance apart so that you can discriminate the students' purposeful choices.

Instructions

Start by having Moe whisper to you. **Moe wants to hear his story again. But this time, I am going to ask you some questions about Moe. You are going to answer the questions by pointing to a picture. The answers are here.** Touch the page in the Student Response Book. **Get ready!**

Read the story "Moe Gets a Pet," stopping to ask the following questions at the end of the designated lines. After asking the question, point to and name the answer choices in the Student Response Book, and then ask the question again. Encourage students who are verbal to point to the correct response and to say the correct response.

Question 1 after viewing the cover: **What do you think this story is going to be about?**
Question 2 from Line 1: **Where did Moe go?**
Question 3 from Line 3: **What did Moe see first?**
Question 4 from line 10: **What pet did Moe get?**

Assisting Students

Prompt If there is no response within 5 seconds, provide the student with a visual cue. For this skill, you might ask Moe to do the visual prompt (e.g., say, **Moe, can you help [student's name] find the answer?**). A visual cue might consist of having Moe tap the correct response. Say, **Moe has shown you the answer. Now I will read the question again, and you show me the answer.** Read the question a second time. If there is still no response within 5 seconds, physically guide the student's hand to the correct response. Say the word as you give the physical cue.

Correction Do not allow students to practice incorrect responses. For a student who can point and is about to point to an incorrect response, physically guide his or her hand to the correct response while verbally reinforcing the response. For students who use eye-gaze and are visually attending to the incorrect response, remove the incorrect response and visually cue them to the correct response.

Objective 6

Demonstrate understanding of syllable segmentation by clapping out syllables in words

Activity

Chunking Words

Materials

- Moe the frog puppet

Tip

A great deal of thought must be given to how a student who is physically challenged will demonstrate this skill. When providing physical cues, make sure the cue can be faded over time. In order for the cue to be faded, the movement you choose must be one the student can create independently (e.g., don't use clapping as a physical cue if the student is unable to clap independently). One way to determine the best movement for the student to use would be to turn on some music, demonstrate moving to the music, and then watch to see what body part the student is able to move independently.

Instructions

Place Moe's mouth near your ear and appear to be listening intently. **Remember, Moe is very shy. He says words in a funny way. He says the sounds in words very slowly. Sometimes it is hard to figure out what he means. Moe wants us to help him. He wants to say the word *excited.* Okeydokey, Moe, you say *excited.*** Listen with concern as Moe says the word *excited.*

Have Moe say, ***Ex...ci...ted,*** slowly dividing it into three syllables.

Moe said *excited* the slow way. He said *ex...ci...ted.* I think he is trying to tell us the syllables he hears in *ex...ci...ted.* Moe, say *excited* again, and we'll clap out the syllables.

Model clapping out the three syllables in the word *excited* as Moe says the word. Make certain that Moe says *excited* slowly, clearly dividing the syllables as he speaks.

Have Moe say, ***Ex...ci...ted.***

Let's say *excited* again slowly and clap out the syllables for Moe. I'll clap and you help me. *Ex...ci...ted.* Help me do that again, boys and girls. Repeat the script.

Have Moe whisper in your ear. **Moe wants to try again with more words. Moe, you choose the next word!**

Have Moe say, ***Jum...ping.***

Repeat the above script using: **jumping, pizza, television.**

Objective 8

Identify letter-sound correspondences

Activity

Letter Sounds Game

Materials

- Moe the frog puppet
- **Level 3 Student Response Book** (pages 222–224)

Tip

When a letter appears between two virgules (/ /), say the sound the letter makes rather than the letter name (e.g., /t/ means to make the sound the letter *t* says).

Instructions

Letter Sounds Game: Part I. Part I reviews the letter *t* and the sound *t* makes. Introduce the activity: **We are going to play the Letter Sounds Game. It's a fun game. Here we go.**

Touch below the *t* on the Sound Presentation page in the Student Response Book and say, **This letter says /t/. The letter *t* says /t/. Touch /t/ with me.** Be sure you are pointing below the t as you say the sound. Don't move your finger until the student points to where you are pointing. **Your turn. Touch /t/.** Give each student the opportunity to touch the *t*.

t

222 ELSB Student Response Book • Lesson 3 • Objective 8: Sound Presentation

Letter Sounds Game: Part II. Part II helps students discriminate the *t* sound from four distractors. Introduce the activity: **Now we get to do the next page of the Letter Sounds Game. Get ready!**

Turn to the Letter-Sound Discrimination page in the Student Response Book. **Touch /t/. Good job touching /t/. The letter *t* says /t/.** Give each student the opportunity to touch the *t*.

Whether students are verbal or nonverbal, encourage them to make the sound for *t*. **This time I will touch the *t* and you say the sound /t/. Ready?** Give each student an opportunity to say /t/.

For review, repeat the above script for the other letters on the page.

Letter Sounds Game: Part III. Part III helps students identify and discriminate *t* when it is the beginning sound in words.

Turn to the Tony Tiger page in the Student Response Book and say, **Our new sound is /t/. Let's practice. Touch /t/. Nice touching /t/. We are going to play a really fun game. First, we will listen to a poem about Tony Tiger. Tony has a terrible toothache that won't go away. Let's read Tony's poem and see if we can hear words that start with /t/.**

Read the following poem one time. While you read, point to the *t* on the Tony Tiger page each time you say a word that begins with *t*.

Tony Tiger

Tony Tiger is sad today.
Tony has a toothache that won't go away.
"Ouch," said Tony,
"I wish someone would take my terrible,
terrible toothache away!"
Tate the zookeeper said, "I think I know the way
to make your terrible toothache go away!"
Off to the dentist went Tony and Tate.
The dentist fixed Tony's tooth.
Now . . . Tony the Tiger feels . . . grrreat!

I will read the poem again and point to /t/ when I hear words that begin with /t/. This time you help me. You touch /t/ when you hear a word that starts with /t/.

Read the poem a second time and encourage students to listen and point to the *t* on the Tony Tiger page when they hear words that begin with /t/. When a student touches the *t* at the appropriate time, give feedback and praise. For example: **Good. The first sound in *today* is /t/.** Note that students may find it difficult to point to the sound every time they hear it, but even pointing to the sound some of the time helps develop their phonemic awareness.

Assisting Students

Prompt If you know a student will not imitate you, guide his or her hand for correct responding. For students who eye-gaze, use a light pointer or tap the answer to get them to focus their gaze on the correct answer.

Correction Touch below the *t* and say, **This sound is /t/. Say /t/ with me. /t/. Say it by yourself. What sound?**

Objective 9

Point to and/or say the first/last sounds in words

Activity

First/Last Sound Game

Materials

- Moe the frog puppet
- **Level 3 Student Response Book** (page 225)

Tips

- When you say the word the "fast way," touch the colored smiley face to focus students, say "Ready," then slash under the word as you say it.
- Stretch the sound when multiple letters appear in the virgules (e.g., /sss/). Note that some sounds cannot be stretched (e.g., /t/).

Instructions

Place Moe's mouth near your ear and appear to be listening. **Moe wants us to get really good at knowing the first sounds in words. Moe has a fun game to play with colored smiling faces to help us hear the first sounds in words. OK, Moe! We are ready to play the First/Last Sound Game.**

Touch the green smiley face on the student page. **Get ready to read the word that comes after the green smiley face. I'll touch and say the first sound /sss/. I'll touch and say the next sound /aaa/. Then I will touch and say the last sound /t/. Say the sounds in this word with me: /sss/ /aaa/ /t/.**

I can say this word the fast way. Ready (put your finger on the smiley face, then say *sat* without segmenting it into sounds), ***sat*. Say this word the fast way with me, *sat*. Yes, *sat*. We said *sat* the fast way.**

Touch the first sound in *sat*. Say, **The first sound in *sat* is /sss/. Touch the first sound in *sat*.** Have a student touch or point to the *s*.

Say the first sound in *sat*. Place emphasis on the beginning sound when you say the word *sat*. **Yes, /sss/ is the first sound in the word *sat*.**

Repeat the script above for: **rat, am, at, tat,** changing the script to match the color of the smiley face and the beginning sound you are focusing on.

Assisting Students

Prompt If you know a student will not imitate you, guide his or her hand for correct responding. For students who eye-gaze, use a light pointer or tap the answer to get them to focus their gaze on the correct answer.

Correction Touch below each sound and say, **This sound is /_____/. Say /_____/ with me. /_____/. Say it by yourself. What sound?**

Objective 10

Identify pictures that begin/end with given sounds

Activity

Finding Pictures with Special Sounds

Materials

- Moe the frog puppet
- **Level 3 Student Response Book** (pages 226–229)

Instructions

Place Moe's mouth near your ear and appear to be listening. **Moe is ready to play his game: Finding Pictures with Special Sounds. The special sounds today are /sss/, /t/, /rrr/, and /mmm/.**

Display the Student Response Book. Point to each picture as you name it (foot, coat, saw, dog), placing emphasis on the first sound in each word.

Say the picture words with me. The first sound in *foot* is /fff/. The first sound in *coat* is /k/. The first sound in *saw* is /sss/. The first sound in *dog* is /d/.

Point to the picture that has /sss/ as its first sound. Show me the picture that starts with /sss/.

Have a student point to the saw. **Yes, the first sound in the word *saw* is /sss/.**

Repeat the above script for each student page. Change the script to match the target sound. The target response (focusing on either /t/, /r/, or /m/) has an asterisk in the list below.

house, moon, *tent, rat
***rake, tape, hat, car**
soap, *mop, fan, door

Give all students 5 seconds to respond after you say, **Show me the picture that starts with _____.**

Assisting Students

Prompt and Correction

If there is no response within 5 seconds, point to the correct response and say, **The first sound in _____ is /_____/. Touch the picture of ______.** If the student does not respond within 5 seconds, physically guide the student's hand to the correct response and say, ______ **starts with /_____/.**

Objective 13

Point to pictures/words representing new vocabulary

Activity

The New Word Game

Materials

- Moe the frog puppet
- **Level 3 Student Response Book** (pages 230–237)

Instructions

Introduce the activity: **We are going to learn about two words to help you with your "My Book About Me" books. One word is *rabbit*. You already know the word *cat*.**

Open the Student Response Book and point to each picture of a rabbit. Say, **This is a rabbit. This is also a rabbit. And this is a rabbit.**

Point to a rabbit as a model. Give each student a turn to point to a picture of a rabbit. Say, **(Student's name), point to a rabbit.** If the student does not point, point to a picture and repeat the direction. If needed, physically guide the student's hand, saying, **This is a rabbit.**

Give each student a turn, pointing to each picture of a rabbit with each turn.

Turn to the next four student pages, which have a rabbit and three distractors, and say, **OK, I'm trying to trick you! Point to the picture of a rabbit.**

Give each student a turn. Use prompts as necessary.

Turn to the next three student pages and repeat the above script with: **cat.**

End the activity by saying, **Great job! Now let's use these words to write another page in your book.**

Assisting Students

Prompt If the student does not point to the picture, physically guide his or her hand, saying, **This is a rabbit (cat).**

Correction If the student points to the wrong picture, model pointing to the correct picture, saying, **This is a rabbit (cat). Now you point to a rabbit (cat).** If the student still does not point to the correct picture, physically guide his or her hand. Give a turn to another classmate, and praise that student for doing it correctly.

Objective 14

Use new vocabulary words and personal information to create a story

Activity

Fun with Writing

Materials

- "My Book About Me" books completed by students in previous lessons
- "My Book About Me, My pet is not a rabbit. My pet is a ______" page in Appendix D
- Pencils, crayons, rubber alphabet stamps, glue
- Pictures of pets
- Pictures of rabbits

Tips

- If a student is not able to write, have the student ask someone to write for him or her. If the student is not verbal, program an AAC device to state, "My pet is not a rabbit. My pet is a ______." You can also create each student's pet response using a word processor and print in a size that will fit on the page. Students can also use the rubber alphabet stamps to stamp their responses.
- If the student is not able to read the sentences in their books, program an AAC device to read the sentences.
- If a student is not able to verbalize for the lesson closing, use an AAC device to say, "Goodbye, Moe."

Instructions

In this activity, students complete another page of their "My Book About Me" books by completing the following: My pet is not a rabbit. My pet is a ______. Students can stamp their responses, write their responses with your assistance, or glue their responses (which have been prepared) on the line.

Introduce the activity: Lay out the "My Book About Me" books, asking students to identify their own. Present the pictures of pets and rabbits.

Say, **Pick a picture of a pet that you have or would really like to have. Then pick a picture of a rabbit.**

Distribute the new "My Book About Me" page. Say, **Touch these sentences and read with me. My pet is not a rabbit. My pet is a ______. Touch the pet that you have or the one that you want to have.** Help them glue the chosen pet picture at the end of the sentence. Then help them write their responses to complete the sentence about their pet. Read the sentences together.

Help the students glue the picture of the chosen rabbit on the page. The students can use a red marker to place an *X* on the rabbit to show their pet is not a rabbit. Encourage all students to use a writing utensil to scribble, write, draw, etc., at the top of the page. Then add the page to their books.

▶ Lesson Closing

Have Moe whisper in your ear. **Boys and girls, Moe said you are incredible workers! Moe will leave now, but he'll be back tomorrow! Say goodbye to Moe!** Have students say goodbye to Moe verbally or by using their AAC devices.

Lesson 4 

Materials

- Moe the frog puppet
- Sight word flashcards: want, he, is, boy
- 2" × 2" Post-it® notes
- **Level 3 Student Response Book** (pages 238–267)
- Magnetic dry erase board and marker
- **All About Moe** easel book: "Moe Gets a Pet" story
- Pictures of pets
- Pictures of birds
- Pencils, crayons, alphabetic rubber stamps, glue
- "My Book About Me" books completed by students in previous lessons
- "My Book About Me, My pet is not a bird. My pet is a ______" page in Appendix D

Optional Materials

- AAC device
- Pointer/light pointer
- Plexiglas® for eye gazing
- Optional pictures or text for AAC device (see Appendix H):
  - Lesson Opening: Good morning, Moe
  - Objective 4: cat
  - Objective 14: My pet is not a bird. My pet is a ______.
  - Lesson Closing: Goodbye, Moe

Tips

- If needed, use the magnetic dry erase board and a marker (or magnetic objects) for reinforcement. Draw a line on the magnet board dividing it into two columns. At the top of the first column, place a picture of the student. At the top of the second column, place a picture of yourself. When a student responds appropriately, congratulate him or her for good work and place a mark on the student side. If a student does not respond appropriately, place a mark on your side. At the end of the lesson, count the marks and find out who had more for that day. Encourage students to participate by being enthusiastic about the marks they received.
- If a student requires an augmentative or alternative communication (AAC) device, preprogram it using the text from the optional materials list.
- All student materials (including AAC overlays and the "My Book About Me" pages) can be printed from Disc 1. Printing from the disc allows you to adapt the materials for students.
- If you are working with a student whose mode of responding is to eye-gaze, the student response options can be printed from Disc 1, laminated, and cut apart. The student choices can be adhered to Plexiglas® with Velcro®. Point to the correct answer after the student gazes to it to provide the watching peers with feedback.

▶ Lesson Opening

Engage the students by saying, **Good morning, Moe!** Have students use an AAC device if needed to say, "Good morning, Moe." **Moe has been waiting for you. Moe is looking really excited this morning. I think he has something to tell you. Why don't you tell them, Moe?** Have Moe whisper in your ear. **OK, Moe. Moe is so excited again, he can hardly talk. He wants you to know that he is going to a special place again. And . . . he says that we will find out where he is going when we read the story today. First, let's practice our flashcard words so we can read the story. Then we will find out where Moe is going.**

Objective 1

Read sight words using time-delay instruction

Activity

Flashcard Game

Materials

- Moe the frog puppet
- Sight word flashcards: want, he, is, boy

Tip

A constant time-delay procedure is used to promote near-errorless responding. If a student is making errors in Round 1, which is the 0-second time-delay round, he or she may need additional practice (outside of this lesson) in imitating your model of choosing the correct response. Using pictures, have the student practice pointing where you point until he or she can do so fluently. If the student makes mistakes in Round 2, which is the 5-second time-delay round, shorten the time before you show the correct answer to 2 seconds. He or she will only have time to answer if certain. The student may also need to practice "wait training" to wait for the response. To do "wait training," use several sheets of different colored paper and say, **Point to the paper.** Have the student wait for you to point to show him or her which sheet.

Instructions

Flashcard Game: Part I. Part I of the Flashcard Game will give students practice saying or pointing to words with guidance.

Round 1: In this round, point to the correct answer as you ask the student to point (0-second time delay).

Lay the sight word flashcards in front of the students. Introduce the activity: **Let's play a game. I'll point to a word, then you point to the same word. Watch me.**

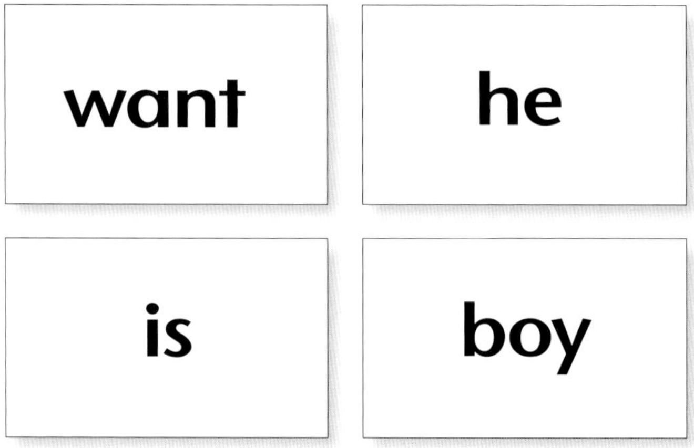

Move the sight word flashcards in front of the first student. Point to the sight word ______ while saying, **This word is ______. (Student name), now you point to ______.**

Be sure you are pointing to the sight word as you say the word. Don't move your finger until the student points to where you are pointing. If you know a student will not imitate you, guide his or her hand for correct responding. For students who eye-gaze, use a light pointer or tap the answer to get them to focus their gaze on the correct answer.

When the student points to ______, say, **Yes, ______.** For students who are verbal, also say, **What word?** and have them say the word.

Wonderful job pointing to the word ______!

Shuffle the sight word flashcards and display them in a new order in front of the next student. In this round, each student takes a turn pointing to the same sight word before moving on to the next sight word.

(Second student's name), point to ______. Be sure you are pointing to ______ as you say the word. Use the same prompt if required.

After each student's turn, shuffle the sight words around so they are not in the same position. Repeat shuffling sight words and pointing to the words until each student has had a turn with each word. Be sure all students are watching during each student's turn to encourage incidental learning.

Round 2: In Round 2 of the Flashcard Game, students point to or say the sight word independently. Moe is ready to help after giving the student up to 5 seconds to initiate a response (a 5-second time delay).

Have Moe whisper in your ear. **Okeydokey, Moe. We can do that. Moe wants you to find the word. He can help you if you are not sure. (Student's name), find the word ______.**

Allow the student 5 seconds to point to the word. After the student finds the word, have Moe point to the same word with the student. **(Student's name), you point with Moe. Thank you for helping, Moe.**

If the student is verbal, have him or her say the word also. If the student does not point, have Moe prompt the answer and restate the word.

Give each student a turn to practice pointing to the sight word you name. Shuffle the sight words and repeat the process for each student with the remaining words. Be sure all students are watching each other's turn.

Awesome playing the Flashcard Game! Moe is learning to read and so are you! Let's play another game.

Assisting Students

Prompt If the student does not point to the word, use Moe to point to the correct word, saying, **Moe pointed to ______. Now you point to ______.** If the student still does not point, physically guide his or her hand.

Correction If the student points to the wrong word, model the correct response by pointing to the correct word and saying, **This is the word ______. Now you point to ______.** If the student still does not point to the correct word, physically guide his or her hand. Give a turn to another classmate, and praise that student for doing it correctly.

Pile on the Praise

Objective 2

Point to the sight words to complete sentences

Activity

Flashcard Game

Materials

- Moe the frog puppet
- Sight word flashcards: want, he, is, boy
- **Level 3 Student Response Book** (pages 238–244)

Instructions

Flashcard Game: Part II. Display the Student Response Book. Place Moe's mouth near your ear and appear to be intently listening. **Moe wants you to read your new word in a sentence. Moe, why do you need to read the words in sentences?** Place Moe's mouth near your ear again. **I see . . . that's what the "big frogs" do! The "big frogs" read words in sentences. Then that's what we want to do!**

Model reading sentence A.1 while pointing to each word in the sentence. Place verbal emphasis on the underlined word. **I <u>want</u> a cat. Listen again. I <u>want</u> a cat.**

Read sentence B.1, pointing to each word. **I _____ a cat.** Point to the blank space.

Place the sight word flashcards in front of a student, using the correct answer and two distractors. **Show Moe which word goes here** (pointing back to the blank space in the sentence). **What word goes here? ______, ______, or ______?**

Allow the student 5 seconds to respond. If the student responds correctly, affirm by saying, **Yes, <u>want</u>. I <u>want</u> a cat.**

Shuffle the sight words and repeat the script with sentences A.2 "**<u>He</u> can swim**" and B.2, as well as sentences A.3 "**Where <u>is</u> my book?**" and B.3, and A.4 "**I like that <u>boy</u>**" and B.4.

Assisting Students

Prompt If the student does not respond within 5 seconds, read sentence A again, placing verbal emphasis on the sight word. Then read sentence B, pausing at the blank space.

______ is the word that goes here. I can find ______. Point to the correct sight word and say, **(Student's name), point to ______ with me. Yes, ______.**

Correction Do not allow students to practice incorrect responses. For a student who can point and is about to point to an incorrect response, physically guide his or her hand to the correct response while verbally reinforcing the response. For students who use eye-gaze and are visually attending to the incorrect response, remove the incorrect response and visually cue them to the correct response.

Objective 3

Point to text as it is read

Activity

Pointing to Words

Materials

- Moe the frog puppet
- "Moe Gets a Pet" story
- **Level 3 Student Response Book** (page 246)

Tips

- Use a wait time of 5 seconds for all responses in this activity. However, students may need longer than 5 seconds initially. In this case, responding within 5 seconds should be viewed as a goal to work toward. Note and track response time for any student for whom you feel it is physically difficult to respond within 5 seconds.
- The goal of text pointing in this level is to have students move left-to-right and top-to-bottom.
- Do not slow your speed of reading to accommodate students' speed of movement. Work toward having students keep pace with your speed of reading as they point to the text.

Instructions

Introduce the activity by saying, **Today we are going to read the story "Moe Gets a Pet."**

While displaying the easel book so all can see, read "Moe Gets a Pet" with enthusiasm, pointing to the text, moving left-to-right and top-to-bottom while you read.

After reading the story, return to the text-pointing page. Say, **Now Moe needs help reading his story. You can help him. I want you to point to each word in the line that I read. Like this.** While displaying the book so all can see, read lines 6–9 of "Moe Gets a Pet." Point to each word in lines 6–9 as you read. Then choose a student to point. Students can point to the text in the story, or you can use the page in the Student Response Book.

(Student's name), your turn! Point to the words for Moe as I read the line. I'm going to show you where to start, and I want you to follow along by pointing to each word as I read it. Show the student where to start pointing by touching the first word.

Repeat for each student, using the lines in the book (or in the Student Response Book).

Let's find out what Moe wants to do next!

Assisting Students

Prompt Modeling for the correct response is already built into the script. A student is given 5 seconds to begin responding. If the student does not initiate a response within 5 seconds, provide a visual cue. A visual cue might be tapping the page in the book and modeling the pointing. If there is still no response within 5 seconds, physically guide the student's hand to point to the words.

Objective 4

Say and/or point to a word to complete a repeated story line

Activity

Hidden Words

Materials

- Moe the frog puppet
- "Moe Gets a Pet" story (prepare for this activity by adhering a Post-it® note to cover the word *cat* highlighted in yellow in story line 7)
- **Level 3 Student Response Book** (page 247)

Tips

- For students who eye-gaze, print the student page from Disc 1 and cut the choices apart. Place the choices a distance apart so that you can discriminate the students' purposeful choices.
- If a student is unable to verbalize, program the AAC device to say the hidden word. Let the student activate the AAC device to say the hidden word and to choose the picture representing the hidden word.

Instructions

Have Moe whisper to you. **Let's play the Hidden Words game! I am going to read a line from the "Moe Gets a Pet" story, and I will point to a word that is hidden** (covered with the Post-it® note). **Get ready!**

Read line 6 from "Moe Gets a Pet," emphasizing the word *cat*.

Read line 7, pausing to remove the Post-it® note. Point to the word *cat* and say, **Cat.**

Again cover the word cat in line 7. Say, **It's your turn, boys and girls! I am going to read these lines, and this time I want you (or a student's name) to say the hidden word. Get ready!**

Read lines 6 and 7, pausing for a student to indicate the hidden word *cat* in line 7. Repeat until all students have had a turn.

Now Moe wants you to point to the picture and the word that tells what the hidden word was. First Moe is going to show you how to do it, and then you will have a turn. I will read the lines again, and he will point to a picture that tells what the uncovered word is. He has three choices here.

Point to the pictures in the Student Response Book and tell the students what the three choices are. Read lines 6 and 7 again, pausing on line 7 for Moe to point to the picture/word representing *cat*. Encourage students to say the uncovered word (use an AAC device for nonverbal students). Repeat the sequence for each student.

Assisting Students

Prompt If there is no response within 5 seconds, provide the student with a visual cue. A visual cue might consist of tapping (or using a light pointer to point to) the correct response. Say the word as you give the visual cue. If there is still no response within 5 seconds, physically guide the student's hand to the correct response. Say the word as you give the physical cue.

Objective 5

Respond to literal questions about a story

Activity

Answering Questions

Materials

- Moe the frog puppet
- "Moe Gets a Pet" story
- **Level 3 Student Response Book** (pages 248–251)

Tips

- Each line is numbered in the story. In this activity, lines 3, 5, and 8 are appropriate places to ask questions. When reading "Moe Gets a Pet," stop to ask questions at lines 3, 5, and 8, and at the end of the story. You do not need to ask each student each question; rather, have students take turns answering the questions.
- For students who eye-gaze, print the student page from Disc 1 and cut the choices apart. Place the choices a distance apart so that you can discriminate the students' purposeful choices.

Instructions

Start by having Moe whisper to you. **Moe wants to hear his story again. But this time, I am going to ask you some questions. You are going to answer the questions by pointing to a picture. The answers are here.** Touch the page in the Student Response Book. **Get ready!**

Read the story "Moe Gets a Pet," stopping to ask the following questions at the end of the designated lines and after reading the entire story. After asking the question, point to and name the answer choices in the Student Response Book, and then ask the question again. Encourage students who are verbal to point to the correct response and to say the correct response.

Question 1 from Line 3: **What was the dog sitting on?**
Question 2 from Line 5: **Who could get only one pet?**
Question 3 from Line 8: **How many pets could Moe get?**
Question 4 after reading the entire story: **What was the story about?**

Assisting Students

Prompt If there is no response within 5 seconds, provide the student with a visual cue. For this skill, you might ask Moe to do the visual prompt (e.g., say, **Moe, can you help [student's name] find the answer?**). A visual cue might consist of having Moe tap the correct response. Say, **Moe has shown you the answer. Now I will read the question again, and you show me the answer.** Read the question a second time. If there is still no response within 5 seconds, physically guide the student's hand to the correct response. Say the word as you give the physical cue.

Correction Do not allow students to practice incorrect responses. For a student who can point and is about to point to an incorrect response, physically guide his or her hand to the correct response while verbally reinforcing the response. For students who use eye-gaze and are visually attending to the incorrect response, remove the incorrect response and visually cue them to the correct response.

Objective 6

Demonstrate understanding of syllable segmentation by clapping out syllables in words

Activity

Chunking Words

Materials

- Moe the frog puppet

Tip

A great deal of thought must be given to how a student who is physically challenged will demonstrate this skill. When providing physical cues, make sure the cue can be faded over time. In order for the cue to be faded, the movement you choose must be one the student can create independently (e.g., don't use clapping as a physical cue if the student is unable to clap independently). One way to determine the best movement for the student to use would be to turn on some music, demonstrate moving to the music, and then watch to see what body part the student is able to move independently.

Instructions

Place Moe's mouth near your ear and appear to be listening intently. **Remember, Moe is very shy. He says words in a funny way. He says the sounds in words very slowly. Sometimes it is hard to figure out what he means. Moe wants us to help him. He wants to say the word *hamburger*. Okeydokey, Moe, you say *hamburger*.** Listen with concern as Moe says the word *hamburger*.

Have Moe say, ***Ham...bur...ger,*** by slowly dividing it into three syllables.

Moe said *hamburger* the slow way. He said *ham...bur...ger*. I think he is trying to tell us the syllables he hears in *ham... bur ...ger*. Moe, say *hamburger* again, and we'll clap out the syllables.

Model clapping out the three syllables in the word *hamburger* as Moe says the word. Make certain that Moe says *hamburger* slowly, clearly dividing the syllables as he speaks.

Have Moe say, ***Ham...bur...ger.***

Let's say *hamburger* again slowly and clap out the syllables for Moe. I'll clap and you help me. *Ham...bur...ger.* Help me do that again, boys and girls. Repeat the script.

Have Moe whisper in your ear. **Moe wants to try again with more words. Moe, you choose the next word!**

Have Moe say, ***In...cre...di...ble.***

Repeat the above script using: **incredible, Moe,** and a **student's name.**

Objective 8

Identify letter-sound correspondences

Activity

Letter Sounds Game

Materials

- Moe the frog puppet
- **Level 3 Student Response Book** (pages 252–254)

Tip

When a letter appears between two virgules (/ /), say the sound the letter makes rather than the letter name (e.g., /t/ means to make the sound the letter *t* says).

Instructions

Letter Sounds Game: Part I. Part I reviews the letter *t* and the sound *t* makes. Introduce the activity: **We are going to play the Letter Sounds Game. It's a fun game. Here we go.**

Touch below the *t* on the Sound Presentation page in the Student Response Book and say, **This letter says /t/. The letter *t* says /t/. Touch /t/ with me.** Be sure you are pointing below the *t* as you say the sound. Don't move your finger until the student points to where you are pointing. **Your turn. Touch /t/.** Give each student an opportunity to touch the *t*.

Letter Sounds Game: Part II. Part II helps students discriminate the *t* sound from four distractors. Introduce the activity: **Now we get to do the next page of the Letter Sounds Game. Get ready!**

Turn to the Letter-Sound Discrimination page in the Student Response Book. **Touch /t/. Good job touching /t/. The letter *t* says /t/.** Give each student an opportunity to touch the *t*.

Whether students are verbal or nonverbal, encourage them to make the sound for *t*. **This time I will touch the *t* and you say the sound /t/. Ready?** Give each student an opportunity to say /t/.

For review, repeat the above script for the other letters on the page.

Letter Sounds Game: Part III. Part III helps students identify and discriminate *t* when it is the beginning sound in words.

Turn to the Tony Tiger page in the Student Response Book and say, **Our sound is /t/. Let's practice. Touch /t/. Nice touching /t/. We are going to play a really fun game. First, we will listen to the poem about Tony Tiger. Tony has a terrible toothache that won't go away. Let's read Tony's poem and see if we can hear words that start with /t/.**

Read the following poem one time. While you read, point to the *t* on the Tony Tiger page each time you say a word that begins with *t*.

Tony Tiger

Tony Tiger is sad today.
Tony has a toothache that won't go away.
"Ouch," said Tony,
"I wish someone would take my terrible,
terrible toothache away!"
Tate the zookeeper said, "I think I know the way
to make your terrible toothache go away!"
Off to the dentist went Tony and Tate.
The dentist fixed Tony's tooth.
Now . . . Tony the Tiger feels . . . grrreat!

I will read the poem again and point to /t/ when I hear words that begin with /t/. This time you help me. You touch /t/ when you hear a word that starts with /t/.

Read the poem a second time and encourage students to listen and point to the *t* on the Tony Tiger page when they hear words that begin with /t/. When a student touches the *t* at the appropriate time, give feedback and praise. For example: **Good. The first sound in *today* is /t/.** Note that students may find it difficult to point to the sound every time they hear it, but even pointing to the sound some of the time helps develop their phonemic awareness.

Assisting Students

Prompt If you know a student will not imitate you, guide his or her hand for correct responding. For students who eye-gaze, use a light pointer or tap the answer to get them to focus their gaze on the correct answer.

Correction Touch below the *t* and say, **This sound is /t/. Say /t/ with me. /t/. Say it by yourself. What sound?**

Objective 9

Point to and/or say the first/last sounds in words

Activity

First/Last Sound Game

Materials

- Moe the frog puppet
- **Level 3 Student Response Book** (page 255)

Tips

- When you say the word the "fast way," touch the colored smiley face to focus students, say "Ready," then slash under the word as you say it.
- Stretch the sound when multiple letters appear in the virgules (e.g., /mmm/). Note that some sounds cannot be stretched (e.g., /t/).

Instructions

Place Moe's mouth near your ear and appear to be listening. **Moe wants us to get really good at knowing the first sounds in words. Moe has a fun game to play with colored smiling faces to help us hear the first sounds in words. OK, Moe! We are ready to play the First/Last Sound Game.**

Touch the green smiley face on the student page. **Get ready to read the word that comes after the green smiley face. I'll touch and say the first sound /mmm/. I'll touch and say the next sound /aaa/. Then I will touch and say the last sound /t/. Say the sounds in this word with me: /mmm/ /aaa/ /t/.**

I can say this word the fast way. Ready (put your finger on the smiley face, then say *mat* without segmenting it into sounds), ***mat.*** **Say this word the fast way with me, *mat.* Yes, *mat.* We said *mat* the fast way.**

Touch the first sound in *mat.* **The first sound in *mat* is /mmm/. Touch the first sound in *mat.*** Have a student touch or point to the ***m.***

Say the first sound in *mat.* Place emphasis on the beginning sound when you say the word *mat.* **Yes, /mmm/ is the first sound in the word *mat.***

Repeat the script above for: **ram, sat, tam, at,** changing the script to match the color of the smiley face and the beginning sound you are focusing on.

Assisting Students

Prompt If you know a student will not imitate you, guide his or her hand for correct responding. For students who eye-gaze, use a light pointer or tap the answer to get them to focus their gaze on the correct answer.

Correction Touch below each sound and say, **This sound is /_____/. Say /_____/ with me. /_____/. Say it by yourself. What sound?**

Objective 10

Identify pictures that begin/end with given sounds

Activity

Finding Pictures with Special Sounds

Materials

- Moe the frog puppet
- **Level 3 Student Response Book** (pages 256–259)

Instructions

Place Moe's mouth near your ear and appear to be listening. **Moe is ready to play his game: Finding Pictures with Special Sounds. The special sounds today are /t/, /rrr/, /mmm/, and /aaa/.**

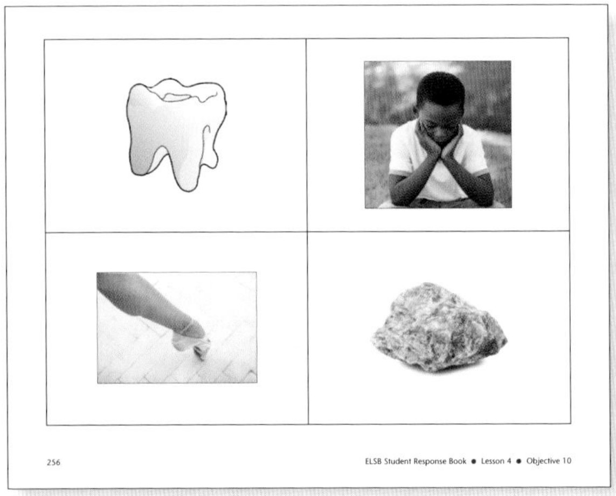

Display the Student Response Book. Point to each picture as you name it (tooth, sad, leg, rock), placing emphasis on the first sound in each word.

Say the picture words with me. The first sound in *tooth* is /t/. The first sound in *sad* is /sss/. The first sound in *leg* is /lll/. The first sound in *rock* is /rrr/.

Point to the picture that has /t/ as its first sound. Show me the picture that starts with /t/.

Have a student point to the tooth. **Yes, the first sound in the word *tooth* is /t/.**

Repeat the above script for each student page. Change the script to match the target sound. The target response (focusing on either /r/, /m/, or /a/) has an asterisk in the list below.

salt, hose, *ring, leaf
fish, *man, girl, rose
ghost, hook, *ant, corn

Give all students 5 seconds to respond after you say, **Show me the picture that starts with ______.**

Assisting Students

Prompt and Correction

If there is no response within 5 seconds, point to the correct response and say, **The first sound in ______ is /_____/. Touch the picture of ______.** If the student does not respond within 5 seconds, physically guide the student's hand to the correct response and say, ______ **starts with /_____/.**

Objective 13

Point to pictures/words representing new vocabulary

Activity

The New Word Game

Materials

- Moe the frog puppet
- **Level 3 Student Response Book** (pages 260–267)

Instructions

Introduce the activity: **We are going to talk about two words to help you with your "My Book About Me" books. One word is new and that word is *bird.* The other word you know, *rabbit.***

Open the Student Response Book and point to each picture of a bird. Say, **This is a bird. This is a bird. And this is a bird.**

Point to a bird as a model. Give each student a turn to point to a picture of a bird. Say, **(Student's name), point to a bird.** If the student does not point, point to a picture and repeat the direction. If needed, physically guide the student's hand, saying, **This is a bird.**

Give each student a turn, pointing to a picture of a bird with each turn.

Turn to the next four student pages, which have a bird and three distractors, and say, **OK, I'm trying to trick you! Point to the picture of a bird.**

Give each student a turn. Use prompts as necessary.

Turn to the next three student pages and repeat the above script with: **rabbit.**

End the activity by saying, **Great job! Now let's use these words to write another page in your book.**

Assisting Students

Prompt If the student does not point to the picture, physically guide his or her hand saying, **This is a bird (rabbit).**

Correction If the student points to the wrong picture, model pointing to the correct picture, saying, **This is a bird (rabbit). Now you point to a bird (rabbit).** If the student still does not point to the correct picture, physically guide his or her hand. Give a turn to another classmate, and praise that student for doing it correctly.

Objective 14

Use new vocabulary words and personal information to create a story

Activity

Fun with Writing

Materials

- "My Book About Me" books completed by students in previous lessons
- "My Book About Me, My pet is not a bird. My pet is a ______" page in Appendix D
- Pencils, crayons, rubber alphabet stamps, glue
- Pictures of pets
- Pictures of birds

Tips

- If a student is not able to write, have the student ask someone to write for him or her. If the student is not verbal, program an AAC device to state, "My pet is not a bird. My pet is a ______." You can also create each student's pet response using a word processor and print in a size that will fit on the page. Students can also use the rubber alphabet stamps to stamp their responses.
- If the student is not able to read the sentences in their books, program an AAC device to read the sentences.
- If a student is not able to verbalize for the lesson closing, use an AAC device to say, "Goodbye, Moe."

Instructions

In this activity, students complete another page of their "My Book About Me" books by completing the following: My pet is not a bird. My pet is a ______. Students can stamp their responses, write their responses with your assistance, or glue their responses (which have been prepared) on the line.

Introduce the activity: **Let's add another page to your book.** Lay out the "My Book About Me" books, asking students to identify their own books. Present the pictures of pets and birds.

Say, **Pick a picture of a pet that you have or would really like to have. Then pick a picture of a bird.**

Distribute the new "My Book About Me" page. Say, **Touch these sentences and read with me. My pet is not a bird. My pet is a ______. Touch the pet that you have or the one that you want to have.** Help them glue the chosen pet picture at the end of the sentence. Then help them write their responses to complete the sentence about their pet. Read the sentences together.

Help the students glue the picture of the chosen bird on the page. The students can use a red marker to place an *X* on the bird to show their pet is not a bird. Encourage all students to use a writing utensil to scribble, write, draw, etc., at the top of the page. Then add the page to their books.

▶ Lesson Closing

Have Moe whisper in your ear. **Boys and girls, Moe said you are just the best workers! Moe will leave now, but he'll be back tomorrow! Say goodbye to Moe!** Have students say goodbye to Moe verbally or by using their AAC devices.

Lesson 5

Materials

- Moe the frog puppet
- Sight word flashcards: want, he, is, boy
- 2" × 2" Post-it® notes
- **Level 3 Student Response Book** (pages 268–297)
- Magnetic dry erase board and marker
- **All About Moe** easel book: "Moe Wants a Pet" and "Moe Gets a Pet" story
- Pictures of pets
- Pencils, crayons, alphabetic rubber stamps, glue
- "My Book About Me" books completed by students in previous lessons
- "My Book About Me, My pet is a ______" page in Appendix D

Optional Materials

- AAC device
- Pointer/light pointer
- Plexiglas® for eye gazing
- Optional pictures or text for AAC device (see Appendix H):
  - Lesson Opening: Hello, Moe
  - Objective 4: one
  - Objective 14: My pet is a ______.
  - Lesson Closing: Goodbye, Moe

Tips

- If needed, use the magnetic dry erase board and a marker (or magnetic objects) for reinforcement. Draw a line on the magnet board dividing it into two columns. At the top of the first column, place a picture of the student. At the top of the second column, place a picture of yourself. When a student responds appropriately, congratulate him or her for good work and place a mark on the student side. If a student does not respond appropriately, place a mark on your side. At the end of the lesson, count the marks and find out who had more for that day. Encourage students to participate by being enthusiastic about the marks they received.

- If a student requires an augmentative or alternative communication (AAC) device, preprogram it using the text from the optional materials list.

- All student materials (including AAC overlays and the "My Book About Me" pages) can be printed from Disc 1. Printing from the disc allows you to adapt the materials for students.

- If you are working with a student whose mode of responding is to eye-gaze, the student response options can be printed from Disc 1, laminated, and cut apart. The student choices can be adhered to Plexiglas® with Velcro®. Point to the correct answer after the student gazes to it to provide the watching peers with feedback.

▶ Lesson Opening

Engage students by saying, **Hello, Moe!** Have students use an AAC device if needed to say, "Hello, Moe." **Moe has been waiting for you. Moe is looking really excited this morning. I think he has something to tell you. Why don't you tell them Moe?** Have Moe whisper in your ear. **OK, Moe. Moe is so excited again, he can hardly talk. He wants you to know that he is going to a special place again. And . . . he says that we will know why when we read the story today. First, let's practice our flashcard words so we can read the story. Then we will find out where Moe is going.**

Objective 1

Read sight words using time-delay instruction

Activity

Flashcard Game

Materials

- Moe the frog puppet
- Sight word flashcards: want, he, is, boy

Tip

A constant time-delay procedure is used to promote near-errorless responding. If a student is making errors in Round 1, which is the 0-second time-delay round, he or she may need additional practice (outside of this lesson) in imitating your model of choosing the correct response. Using pictures, have the student practice pointing where you point until he or she can do so fluently. If the student makes mistakes in Round 2, which is the 5-second time-delay round, shorten the time before you show the correct answer to 2 seconds. He or she will only have time to answer if certain. The student may also need to practice "wait training" to wait for the response. To do "wait training," use several sheets of different colored paper and say, **Point to the paper.** Have the student wait for you to point to show him or her which sheet.

Instructions

Flashcard Game: Part I. Part I of the Flashcard Game will give students practice saying or pointing to words with guidance.

Round 1: In this round, point to the correct answer as you ask the student to point (0-second time delay).

Lay the sight word flashcards in front of the students. Introduce the activity: **Let's play a game. I'll point to a word, then you point to the same word. Watch me.**

want	he
is	boy

Move the sight word flashcards in front of the first student. Point to the sight word ______ while saying, **This word is ______. (Student name), now you point to ______.**

Be sure you are pointing to the sight word as you say the word. Don't move your finger until the student points to where you are pointing. If you know a student will not imitate you, guide his or her hand for correct responding. For students who eye-gaze, use a light pointer or tap the answer to get them to focus their gaze on the correct answer.

When the student points to ______, say, **Yes, ______.** For students who are verbal, also say, **What word?** and have them say the word.

Wonderful job pointing to the word ______!

Shuffle the sight word flashcards and display them in a new order in front of the next student. In this round, each student takes a turn pointing to the same sight word before moving on to the next sight word.

(Second student's name), point to ______. Be sure you are pointing to ______ as you say the word. Use the same prompt if required.

After each student's turn, shuffle the sight words around so they are not in the same position. Repeat shuffling sight words and pointing to the words until each student has had a turn with each word. Be sure all students are watching during each student's turn to encourage incidental learning.

Round 2: In Round 2 of the Flashcard Game, students point to or say the sight word independently. Moe is ready to help after giving the student up to 5 seconds to initiate a response (a 5-second time delay).

Have Moe whisper in your ear. **Okeydokey, Moe. We can do that. Moe wants you to find the word. He can help you if you are not sure. (Student's name), find the word ______.**

Allow the student 5 seconds to point to the word. After the student finds the word, have Moe point to the same word with the student. **(Student's name), you point with Moe. Thank you for helping, Moe.**

If the student is verbal, have him or her say the word also. If the student does not point, have Moe prompt the answer and restate the word.

Give each student a turn to practice pointing to the sight word you name. Shuffle the sight words and repeat the process for each student with the remaining words. Be sure all students are watching each other's turn.

Awesome playing the Flashcard Game! Moe is learning to read and so are you! Let's play the next game.

Assisting Students

Prompt If the student does not point to the word, use Moe to point to the correct word, saying, **Moe pointed to ______. Now you point to ______.** If the student still does not point, physically guide his or her hand.

Correction If the student points to the wrong word, model the correct response by pointing to the correct word and saying, **This is the word ______. Now you point to ______.** If the student still does not point to the correct word, physically guide his or her hand. Give a turn to another classmate, and praise that student for doing it correctly.

Pile on the Praise

Objective 2

Point to the sight words to complete sentences

Activity

Flashcard Game

Materials

- Moe the frog puppet
- Sight word flashcards: want, he, is, boy
- **Level 3 Student Response Book** (pages 268–275)

Instructions

Flashcard Game: Part II. Display the Student Response Book. Place Moe's mouth near your ear and appear to be intently listening. **Moe wants you to read your new word in a sentence. Moe, why do you need to read the words in sentences?** Place Moe's mouth near your ear again. **I see . . . that's what the "big frogs" do! The "big frogs" read words in sentences. Then that's what we want to do!**

Model reading sentence A.1 while pointing to each word in the sentence. Place verbal emphasis on the underlined word. **I don't <u>want</u> to play. Listen again. I don't <u>want</u> to play.**

Read sentence B.1, pointing to each word. **I don't ______ to play.** Point to the blank space.

Place the sight word flashcards in front of a student, using the correct answer and two distractors. **Show Moe which word goes here** (pointing back to the blank space in the sentence). **What word goes here? ______, ______, or ______?**

Allow the student 5 seconds to respond. If the student responds correctly, affirm by saying, **Yes, <u>want</u>. I don't <u>want</u> to play.**

Shuffle the sight words and repeat the script with sentences A.2 "**<u>He</u> is going to school**"and B.2, as well as sentences A.3 "**She <u>is</u> going to the park**" and B.3, and A.4 "**That <u>boy</u> can sing**" and B.4.

Assisting Students

Prompt If the student does not respond within 5 seconds, read sentence A again, placing verbal emphasis on the sight word. Then read sentence B, pausing at the blank space.

______ is the word that goes here. I can find ______. Point to the correct sight word and say, **(Student's name), point to ______ with me. Yes, ______.**

Correction Do not allow students to practice incorrect responses. For a student who can point and is about to point to an incorrect response, physically guide his or her hand to the correct response while verbally reinforcing the response. For students who use eye-gaze and are visually attending to the incorrect response, remove the incorrect response and visually cue them to the correct response.

Objective 3

Point to text as it is read

Activity

Pointing to Words

Materials

- Moe the frog puppet
- "Moe Wants a Pet" and "Moe Gets a Pet" stories
- **Level 3 Student Response Book** (page 276)

Tips

- Use a wait time of 5 seconds for all responses in this activity. However, students may need longer than 5 seconds initially. In this case, responding within 5 seconds should be viewed as a goal to work toward. Note and track response time for any student for whom you feel it is physically difficult to respond within 5 seconds.
- The goal of text pointing in this level is to have students move left-to-right and top-to-bottom.
- Do not slow your speed of reading to accommodate students' speed of movement. Work toward having students keep pace with your speed of reading as they point to the text.

Instructions

Introduce the activity by saying, **Today we are going to read the stories "Moe Wants a Pet" and "Moe Gets a Pet."**

While displaying the easel book so all can see, read "Moe Wants a Pet" with enthusiasm, pointing to the text, moving left-to-right and top-to-bottom while you read. Then read "Moe Gets a Pet" with enthusiasm, also pointing to each word as you read.

After reading the story, return to the text-pointing page. Say, **Now Moe needs help reading "Moe Gets a Pet." You can help him. I want you to point to each word in the lines that I read, like this.** While displaying "Moe Gets a Pet" so all can see, read lines 8–11. Point to each word in lines 8–11 as you read. Then choose a student to point. Students can point to the text in the story, or you can use the page in the Student Response Book.

(Student's name), your turn! Point to the words for Moe as I read the line. I'm going to show you where to start, and I want you to follow along by pointing to each word as I read it. Show the student where to start pointing by touching the first word.

Repeat for each student, using the lines in the book (or in the Student Response Book).

Let's find out what Moe wants to do next!

Assisting Students

Prompt Modeling for the correct response is already built into the script. A student is given 5 seconds to begin responding. If the student does not initiate a response within 5 seconds, provide a visual cue. A visual cue might be tapping the page in the book and modeling the pointing. If there is still no response within 5 seconds, physically guide the student's hand to point to the words.

Objective 4

Say and/or point to a word to complete a repeated story line

Activity

Hidden Words

Materials

- Moe the frog puppet
- "Moe Gets a Pet" story (prepare for this activity by adhering a Post-it® note to cover the word *one* highlighted in yellow in story line 9)
- **Level 3 Student Response Book** (page 277)

Tips

- For students who eye-gaze, print the student page from Disc 1 and cut the choices apart. Place the choices a distance apart so that you can discriminate the students' purposeful choices.
- If a student is unable to verbalize, program the AAC device to say the hidden word. Let the student activate the AAC device to say the hidden word and to choose the picture representing the hidden word.

Instructions

Have Moe whisper to you. **Let's play the Hidden Words game! I am going to read a line from the "Moe Gets a Pet" story, and I will point to a word that is hidden** (covered with the Post-it® note). **Get ready!**

Read line 8 from "Moe Gets a Pet," emphasizing the word *one.*

Read line 9, pausing to remove the Post-it® note. Point to the word *one* and say, **One.**

Again cover the word *one* in line 8. Say, **It's your turn, boys and girls! I am going to read these lines, and this time I want you (or a student's name) to say the hidden word. Get ready!**

Read lines 8 and 9, pausing for a student to indicate the hidden word *one* in line 9. Uncover the word when students say it. Repeat until all students have had a turn.

Now Moe wants you to point to the picture and the word that tells what the hidden word was. First Moe is going to show you how to do it, and then you will have a turn. I will read the lines again, and he will point to a picture that tells what the uncovered word is. He has three choices here.

Point to the pictures in the Student Response Book and tell the students what the three choices are. Read lines 8 and 9 again, pausing on line 9 for Moe to point to the picture/word representing *one.* Encourage students to say the uncovered word (use an AAC device for nonverbal students). Repeat the sequence for each student.

Assisting Students

Prompt If there is no response within 5 seconds, provide the student with a visual cue. A visual cue might consist of tapping (or using a light pointer to point to) the correct response. Say the word as you give the visual cue. If there is still no response within 5 seconds, physically guide the student's hand to the correct response. Say the word as you give the physical cue.

Objective 5

Respond to literal questions about a story

Activity

Answering Questions

Materials

- Moe the frog puppet
- "Moe Wants a Pet" and "Moe Gets a Pet" stories
- **Level 3 Student Response Book** (pages 278–281)

Tips

- Each line is numbered in the story. In this activity, lines 2 and 7 in "Moe Wants a Pet" and lines 9 and 10 in "Moe Gets a Pet" are appropriate places to ask questions. When reading, stop to ask questions at lines 2 and 7 in "Moe Wants a Pet" and lines 9 and 10 in "Moe Gets a Pet." You do not need to ask each student each question; rather, have students take turns answering the questions.
- For students who eye-gaze, print the student page from Disc 1 and cut the choices apart. Place the choices a distance apart so that you can discriminate the students' purposeful choices.

Instructions

Start by having Moe whisper to you. **Moe wants to hear both of his stories again. But this time, I am going to ask you some questions about Moe. You are going to answer the questions by pointing to a picture. The answers are here.** Touch the page in the Student Response Book. **Get ready!**

Read the stories, stopping to ask the following questions at the end of the designated lines. After asking the question, point to and name the answer choices in the Student Response Book, and then ask the question again. Encourage students who are verbal to point to the correct response and to say the correct response.

"Moe Wants a Pet"
Question 1 from Lines 1 and 2: **Who is going to the pet store?**
Question 2 from Line 7: **What pet does Moe want?**

"Moe Gets a Pet"
Question 3 from Line 9: **How many pets Moe get?**
Question 4 from Line 10: **What pet did Moe get?**

Assisting Students

Prompt If there is no response within 5 seconds, provide the student with a visual cue. For this skill, you might ask Moe to do the visual prompt (e.g., say, **Moe, can you help [student's name] find the answer?**). A visual cue might consist of having Moe tap the correct response. Say, **Moe has shown you the answer. Now I will read the question again, and you show me the answer.** Read the question a second time. If there is still no response within 5 seconds, physically guide the student's hand to the correct response. Say the word as you give the physical cue.

Correction Do not allow students to practice incorrect responses. For a student who can point and is about to point to an incorrect response, physically guide his or her hand to the correct response while verbally reinforcing the response. For students who use eye-gaze and are visually attending to the incorrect response, remove the incorrect response and visually cue them to the correct response.

Objective 6

Demonstrate understanding of syllable segmentation by clapping out syllables in words

Activity

Chunking Words

Materials

- Moe the frog puppet

Tip

A great deal of thought must be given to how a student who is physically challenged will demonstrate this skill. When providing physical cues, make sure the cue can be faded over time. In order for the cue to be faded, the movement you choose must be one the student can create independently (e.g., don't use clapping as a physical cue if the student is unable to clap independently). One way to determine the best movement for the student to use would be to turn on some music, demonstrate moving to the music, and then watch to see what body part the student is able to move independently.

Instructions

Place Moe's mouth near your ear and appear to be listening intently. **Remember, Moe is very shy. He says words in a funny way. He says the sounds in words very slowly. Sometimes it is hard to figure out what he means. Moe wants us to help him. He wants to say the word *happy*. Okeydokey, Moe, you say *happy*.** Listen with concern as Moe says the word *happy*.

Have Moe say, ***Ha...ppy,*** slowly dividing it into two syllables.

Moe said *happy* the slow way. He said *ha...ppy*. I think he is trying to tell us the syllables he hears in *ha...ppy*. Moe, say *happy* again, and we'll clap out the syllables.

Model clapping out the two syllables in the word *happy* as Moe says the word. Make certain that Moe says *happy* slowly, clearly dividing the syllables as he speaks.

Have Moe say, ***Ha...ppy.***

Let's say *happy* again slowly and clap out the syllables for Moe. I'll clap and you help me. *Ha...ppy*. Help me do that again, boys and girls. Repeat the script.

Have Moe whisper in your ear. **Moe wants to try again with more words. Moe, you choose the next word!**

Have Moe say, ***Ex...ci...ted.***

Repeat the above script using: **excited, television,** and **your name.**

Objective 8

Identify letter-sound correspondences

Activity

Letter Sounds Game

Materials

- Moe the frog puppet
- **Level 3 Student Response Book** (pages 282–284)

Tip

When a letter appears between two virgules (/ /), say the sound the letter makes rather than the letter name (e.g., /a/ means to make the sound *a* says). Stretch the sound when multiple letters (e.g., /aaa/) appear within the virgules.

Instructions

Letter Sounds Game: Part I. Part I reviews the letter *a* and the sound short *a* makes, as in *alligator*. Introduce the activity: **We are going to play the Letter Sounds Game. It's a fun game. Here we go.**

Touch below the *a* on the Sound Presentation page in the Student Response Book and say, **This letter says /aaa/. The letter *a* says /aaa/. Touch /aaa/ with me.** Be sure you are pointing below the *a* as you say the sound. Don't move your finger until the student points to where you are pointing. **Your turn. Touch /aaa/.** Give each student an opportunity to touch the *a*.

Letter Sounds Game: Part II. Part II helps students discriminate the short *a* sound from four distractors. Introduce the activity: **Now we get to do the next page of the Letter Sounds Game. Get ready!**

Turn to the Letter-Sound Discrimination page in the Student Response Book. **Touch /aaa/. Good job touching /aaa/. The letter *a* says /aaa/.** Give each student an opportunity to touch the *a*.

Whether students are verbal or nonverbal, encourage them to make the sound for short *a*. **This time I will touch the *a* and you say the sound /aaa/. Ready?** Give each student an opportunity to say short /a/.

For review, repeat the above script for the other sounds.

Letter Sounds Game: Part III. Part III helps students identify and discriminate the short *a* when it is the beginning sound in words.

Turn to the Aggie and Ally page in the Student Response Book and say, **Our sound is /aaa/. Let's practice. Touch /aaa/. Nice touching /aaa/. We are going to play a really fun game. First, we will listen to the poem about Aggie and Ally. Remember, Aggie and Ally are alligators and they love words that start with /aaa/. Let's read their poem and see if we can hear words that start with /aaa/.**

Read the poem on page 150 one time. While you read, point to the *a* on the Aggie and Ally page each time you say a word that begins with *a*.

a

Aggie and Ally Alligator

284 ELSB Student Response Book • Lesson 5 • Objective 8: Aggie and Ally

Aggie and Ally

Aggie the **a**lligator lives down in the bay
with her sister named **A**lly on
"**A**lligator Way."
Aggie **a**nd **A**lly work in the morning
and play in the **a**fternoon.
They play a game called "**A**fternoon Moon."
They swim up in the water **a**nd go snap, snap, snap.
They swim down in the water **a**nd go whap, whap, whap!
Then **A**ggie **A**lligator **a**nd **A**lly **A**lligator
take a long, long **a**fternoon nap!

I will read the poem again and point to /aaa/ when I hear words that begin with /aaa/. This time you help me. You touch /aaa/ when you hear a word that starts with /aaa/.

Read the poem a second time and encourage students to listen and point to the *a* on the Aggie and Ally page when they hear words that begin with /a/. Stretch the beginning sound to emphasize the *a*. When a student touches the *a* at the appropriate time, give feedback and praise. Stretch the beginning sound to emphasize the *a*. For example: **Good. The first sound in *alligator* is /aaa/.** Note that students may find it difficult to point to the sound every time they hear it, but even pointing to the sound some of the time helps develop their phonemic awareness.

Assisting Students

Prompt If you know a student will not imitate you, guide his or her hand for correct responding. For students who eye-gaze, use a light pointer or tap the answer to get them to focus their gaze on the correct answer.

Correction Touch below the *a* and say, **This sound is /aaa/. Say /aaa/ with me. /aaa/. Say it by yourself. What sound?**

Objective 9

Point to and/or say the first/last sounds in words

Activity

First/Last Sound Game

Materials

- Moe the frog puppet
- **Level 3 Student Response Book** (page 285)

Tips

- When you say the word the "fast way," touch the colored smiley face to focus students, say "Ready," then slash under the word as you say it.
- Stretch the sound when multiple letters appear in the virgules (e.g., /sss/). Note that some sounds cannot be stretched (e.g., /t/).

Instructions

Place Moe's mouth near your ear and appear to be listening. **Moe wants us to get really good at knowing the first sounds in words. Moe has a fun game to play with colored smiling faces to help us hear the first sounds in words. OK, Moe! We are ready to play the First/Last Sound Game.**

Touch the green smiley face on the student page. **Get ready to read the word that comes after the green smiley face. I'll touch and say the first sound /sss/. I will touch and say the next sound /aaa/. Then I will touch and say the last sound /t/.**

Say the sounds in this word with me: /sss/ /aaa/ /t/.

I can say this word the fast way. Ready (put your finger on the smiley face, then say *sat* without segmenting it into sounds), ***sat*. Say this word the fast way with me, *sat*. Yes, *sat*. We said *sat* the fast way.**

Touch the first sound in *sat*. Say, **The first sound in *sat* is /sss/. Touch the first sound in *sat*.** Have a student touch or point to the *s*.

Say the first sound in *sat*. Place emphasis on the beginning sound when you say the word *sat*. **Yes, /sss/ is the first sound in the word *sat*.**

Repeat the script above for: **ran, mat, am, tam,** changing the script to match the color of the smiley face and the beginning sound you are focusing on.

Assisting Students

Prompt If you know a student will not imitate you, guide his or her hand for correct responding. For students who eye-gaze, use a light pointer or tap the answer to get them to focus their gaze on the correct answer.

Correction Touch below each sound and say, **This sound is /____/. Say /____/ with me. /____/. Say it by yourself. What sound?**

Objective 10

Identify pictures that begin/end with given sounds

Activity

Finding Pictures with Special Sounds

Materials

- Moe the frog puppet
- **Level 3 Student Response Book** (pages 286–289)

Instructions

Place Moe's mouth near your ear and appear to be listening. **Moe is ready to play his game: Finding Pictures with Special Sounds. The special sounds today are /sss/, /rrr/, /t/, and /aaa/.**

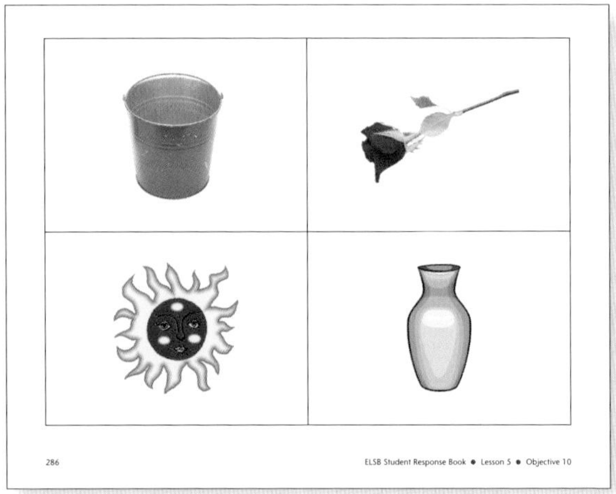

Display the Student Response Book. Point to each picture as you name it (pail, rose, sun, vase), placing emphasis on the first sound in each word.

Say the picture words with me. The first sound in *pail* is /p/. The first sound in *rose* is /rrr/. The first sound in *sun* is /sss/. The first sound in *vase* is /vvv/.

Point to the picture that has /sss/ as its first sound. Show me the picture that starts with /sss/.

Have a student point to the sun. **Yes, the first sound in the word *sun* is /sss/.**

Repeat the above script for each student page. Change the script to match the target sound. The target response (focusing on either /r/, /t/, or /a/) has an asterisk in the list below.

***rain, bug, bird, cat**
pea, *teeth, dog, fan
key, map, ball, *apple

Give all students 5 seconds to respond after you say, **Show me the picture that starts with _____.**

Assisting Students

Prompt and Correction

If there is no response within 5 seconds, point to the correct response and say, **The first sound in _____ is /_____/. Touch the picture of _____.** If the student does not respond within 5 seconds, physically guide the student's hand to the correct response and say, _____ **starts with /_____/.**

Objective 13

Point to pictures/words representing new vocabulary

Activity

The New Word Game

Materials

- Moe the frog puppet
- **Level 3 Student Response Book** (pages 290–297)

Instructions

Introduce the activity: **We are going to talk about two words to help you with your "My Book About Me" books. Your words today are *dog* and *bird*.**

Open the Student Response Book and point to each picture of a dog. Say, **This is a dog. This is a dog. And this is a dog.**

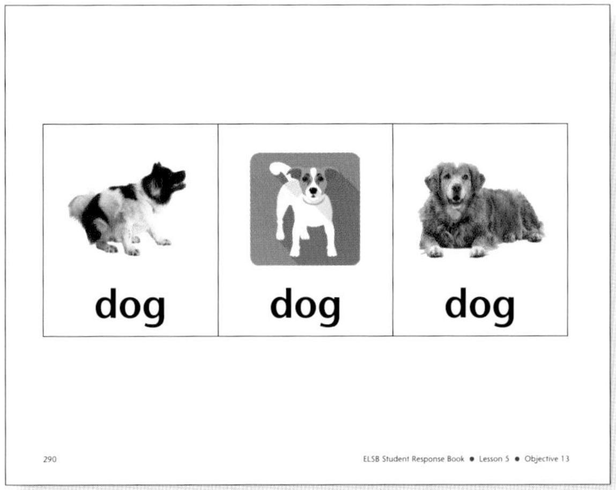

Give each student a turn to point to a picture of a dog. Say, **(Student's name), point to a dog.** If the student does not point, point to a picture and repeat the question. If needed, physically guide the student's hand, saying, **This is a dog.**

Give each student a turn, pointing to a picture of a dog with each turn.

Turn to the next three student pages, which have a dog and three distractors, and say, **OK, I'm trying to trick you! Point to the picture of a dog.**

Give each student a turn. Use prompts as necessary.

Turn to the next four student pages and repeat the above script with: **bird.**

End the activity by saying, **Great job! Now let's use these words to write another page in your book.**

Assisting Students

Prompt If the student does not point to the picture, physically guide his or her hand, saying, **This is a dog (bird).**

Correction If the student points to the wrong picture, model pointing to the correct picture and saying, **This is a dog (bird). Now you point to a dog (bird).** If the student still does not point to the correct picture, physically guide his or her hand. Give a turn to another classmate, and praise that student for doing it correctly.

Objective 14

Use new vocabulary words and personal information to create a story

Activity

Fun with Writing

Materials

- "My Book About Me" books completed by students in previous lessons
- "My Book About Me, My pet is a ______" page in Appendix D
- Pencils, crayons, rubber alphabet stamps, glue
- Pictures of pets

Tips

- If a student is not able to write, have the student ask someone to write for him or her. If the student is not verbal, program an AAC device to state, "My pet is a ______." You can also create each student's pet response using a word processor and print in a size that will fit on the page. Students can also use the rubber alphabet stamps to stamp their responses.
- If the student is not able to read the sentences in their books, program an AAC device to read the sentences or to read the new sentence.
- If a student is not able to verbalize for the lesson closing, use an AAC device to say, "Goodbye, Moe."

Instructions

In this activity, students complete another page of their "My Book About Me" books by completing the following: My pet is a ______. Students can stamp their responses, write their responses with your assistance, or glue their responses (which have been prepared) on the line.

Introduce the activity: Lay out the "My Book About Me" books, asking students to identify their own. Present the pictures of pets.

Say, **Pick a picture of a pet that you have or would really like to have.**

Distribute the new "My Book About Me" page. Say, **Touch this sentence and read with me. My pet is a ______. Touch the pet that you have or the one that you want to have.** Help them glue the chosen pet picture at the end of the sentence. Then help them write their responses to complete the sentence about their pet. Read the sentences together. Encourage all students to use a writing utensil to scribble, write, draw, etc., at the top of the page. Then add the page to their books.

▶ Lesson Closing

Have Moe whisper in your ear. **Boys and girls, Moe said you are all incredible! Moe will leave now, but he'll be back tomorrow! Say goodbye to Moe!** Have students say goodbye to Moe verbally or by using their AAC devices.